PRESS ON!

A DEVOTIONAL GUIDE FOR CROSS-CULTURAL WORKERS
AND THOSE WHO CARE ABOUT THEM

PRESS ON!

What the missionary journeys of
James Gribble teach us about *prayer*,
perseverance, and the *ultimate prize*

DAVE GUILES

Foreword by Sherwood Lingenfelter

Dedicated to the faithful, self-sacrificing, and hardworking members of Encompass World Partners, who for over 120 years have labored among the least-reached in dozens of countries around the globe. Someday I hope we can tell your amazing stories!

"I press on . . ."

THE APOSTLE PAUL,
TO THE YOUNG BELIEVERS AT PHILIPPI

"I long to go to the darkest and most densely populated region, to a place where not only has the Gospel never been preached, but where no one else plans to preach it."

JAMES GRIBBLE,
CAPE TOWN, SOUTH AFRICA, 1914

TABLE OF CONTENTS

FOREWORD

SINCE THE DAY OF PENTECOST, the Holy Spirit has touched men and women with God's power, overturned their priorities for living, and called them on impossible journeys to proclaim the incredible news of the death and resurrection of Jesus Christ. This book is a reflection on how one man, James Gribble, and two women, Florence Newberry Gribble and Estella Myers—called by God to embark together on such an impossible journey in 1918—lived into the promises of God and trusted God to evangelize some of the most resistant and least-reached people groups on earth.

The purpose of the book, however, is not history, but rather deep reflection on how people faced with impossible circumstances—war, shipwreck, poverty, implacable governments, endless waiting, malaria, flu, dysentery, theft, people with no interest in the gospel, and even death of coworkers—sought direction from God through Scripture and prayer in each crisis. They went out with great hope and expectations, and when hope was shattered, and expectation was gone, they persisted in their calling, believing that the God who called them would fulfill His promises. James is the primary narrator of this story, reflecting daily on how God—and his companions Florence and Estella, as well as the body of Christ at home—sustained them on this impossible journey. He also grieves when others who embraced his vision and joined them along the way either died from the unrelenting malaria or gave up during the long sickness, waiting, and loss of hope.

Mission today has undergone radical change. The vast percentage of unreached peoples live in modern cities around the globe, but seemingly impossible obstacles of danger, disease, and apathy continue to destroy hope and deny the expectations of twenty-first-century men and women called by God as servants to declare that "the kingdom of God is near." My Chinese friends—living sacrificially in a North African city, loving their neighbors, serving the local Muslim community, and declaring the Good News to any who will listen—suffer from resistant neighbors and fear of those in government and community who hate Christians. My Palestinian friend who seeks to love and care for nine hundred refugee families living in Jordan suffers from the lack of funds, the overwhelming needs of families, the death of both refugees and colleagues, and the governments that harass him at every border as he seeks to bring the Good News of Jesus. My former students in America who were called in 1990 to proclaim Christ to Muslim communities in Asia continue today to travel from village to village, town to town, sharing medical care, love for these neighbors, and the Good News; and seem to be endlessly waiting for the Holy Spirit to open eyes and hearts and bring in His harvest.

If you, like my friends above, have accepted God's call to proclaim Christ in the most densely populated urban centers of the globe, or if you, like me, support others that God has called to such places, Dave Guiles has written this book for us. I first got to know Dave and Sue Guiles as missionary candidates in 1985, when they were preparing to serve on a church planting team in the cities of Argentina. As a member of the mission board under which they served, I rejoiced at how they followed God's call and matured as effective church planters, empowering Argentinians to share the gospel and make disciples in their urban family networks. I was part of the board in 2000 that appointed Dave as executive director of Encompass World Partners, where he has since served for twenty years. I have listened to Dave publicly reflect on the critical moments in James Gribble's missionary journey as Dave has sought to mobilize a new generation of missionaries for Encompass and to challenge congregations to support these men and women for the mission of God in the twenty-first century.

This book is Dave's gift to us about what God has taught him from Gribble's letters and from the narrative of Gribble's wife, Florence, regarding their team ministry in Central Africa. As is typical of Dave's leadership and ministry, each chapter begins with selected Scripture, upon which Dave invites us, the readers, to reflect concerning a particular part of the Gribble missionary story. Each critical moment in Gribble's experience enables us to reflect upon similar moments in our own stories—responding to God's call, taking risks "to follow" that seem insane to others, being surprised when God's way is not our plan, suffering while we wait for God's action, and even despairing when we lose precious members of our teams. This book is about trusting God when nothing seems to work the way we plan or hope, and watching God do mission God's way.

My wife, Judith, and I have taken this forty-two-day journey of reflection—Scripture, the Gribble story, our present journey with God—combined with prayer and action to trust God in our current "critical moments" of following Jesus. We invite you to take this journey with someone else with whom you have a personal or ministry relationship, and pray that God, through His Spirit, will enable you together to take your next steps in God's mission for His global church. My prayer is that this book will enable you to reflect deeply upon what God has already done in your journey, and in gratitude, live into the unfulfilled promises that God has made to you through His word (Hebrews 11:13).

Sherwood Lingenfelter
SENIOR PROFESSOR OF ANTHROPOLOGY AND PROVOST EMERITUS
FULLER THEOLOGICAL SEMINARY

INTRODUCTION

In 1996, a coalition of mission agencies cooperated in producing a remarkable map called the Status of Global Evangelization. They used the color red to highlight regions where Jesus and His Church are relatively unknown. There's a lot of red ink on the map, and most of it falls within that area we commonly call the 10/40 Window. Their map was a cry for help to mobilize prayer and missionary deployment in the least-evangelized regions of our world. Other colors—pink, yellow, and green—were more encouraging, as they revealed increasing levels of success in making disciples and planting churches.

Harder to locate was the color purple. The five small purple spots on a big map were easy to overlook by casual observers. What did they represent? The *highest* degree of response to the Good News of Jesus Christ. Two were located in North America, and one each in South America and Asia.

One purple spot, by far the largest, was centered on the western half of the present-day Central African Republic. At the time the map was published, it was considered the most evangelized region on planet earth.

Yet less than a century earlier, pioneer missionary James Gribble wrote about this very region:

> I long to go to the darkest and most densely populated
> region, to a place where not only has the Gospel never
> been preached, but where no one else plans to preach it. In
> the vast section to which we hope to go, the influence of
> Islam is yet practically non-existent. What a barrier to its
> onward tread a line of stations across that beautiful country
> would be! That long, grass country far beyond the bounds
> of civilization—how it beckons me on! The people are said
> to be agriculturists, hunters, and fishermen. They have no
> cattle, few sheep, and no fowls. They are said to be fierce
> cannibals, but that may be at least a partial exaggeration.

This is the story of James Gribble and the team that helped him penetrate the very heart of Africa with the gospel of Christ. It is part personal journal, part pioneer adventure, and part love story, but above all, it is a story of sacrifice and perseverance in the face of overwhelming obstacles. I believe it ranks among the most inspiring stories of the modern era of missions. And I think you will too!

I should point out that this isn't the first attempt to tell this remarkable story. So why another book about James Gribble? Most other versions are out of print and written in styles somewhat inaccessible to readers today. I hope this book is both easy to find and easy to read. But more importantly, as a former missionary myself, I see frequent and amazing parallels between the experiences of James Gribble and others who have left home and crossed geographic, cultural, and linguistic boundaries to make disciples among the nations. That's why I've chosen to write this story primarily with deployed missionaries in mind.

Following the format of a six-week devotional, each day begins with an opportunity to reflect upon Scripture, then moves to a dramatic retelling of an incident from James' life, and concludes with a series of questions for personal reflection. My earnest prayer is that this material serves to challenge, encourage, and even inspire missionaries to "keep their hands to the plow and not look back."

But what about the rest of us? Does James Gribble still speak to non-missionaries today? I sincerely hope so! And it's with that in mind that I invite others to read this book as though you're peering over the shoulders of the cross-cultural missionaries you know, love, and support. I believe this story will inspire you to renew your own passion and commitment to make disciples of Jesus Christ, whether across the street or in the far-flung corners of our world!

Dave Guiles
ATLANTA, GEORGIA
MISSIONARY TO ARGENTINA (1987–1999)
EXECUTIVE DIRECTOR OF ENCOMPASS WORLD PARTNERS
(2000–PRESENT)

What's the 10/40 Window? According to the Joshua Project (see joshuaproject.org), "The 10/40 Window is the rectangular area of North Africa, the Middle East and Asia approximately between 10 degrees north and 40 degrees north latitude. The 10/40 Window is often called 'The Resistant Belt' and includes the majority of the world's Muslims, Hindus, and Buddhists." As of this moment, over 5.1 billion people reside in this region, scattered among 8,918 different ethnic groups. Over 6,200 of those groups are considered "least-reached." Anyone who cares about the Great Commission of Jesus Christ must be sobered upon considering the spiritual plight of the billions of people who reside there.

EMBRACING THE CALL

PHILADELPHIA, FEBRUARY 4–5, 1904

I have appeared to you for this purpose,
to appoint you as a servant and witness.

ACTS 26:16

Left: Trolley car similar to what James Gribble drove in the streets of Philadelphia, shortly after leaving the family farm to seek his fortune. *Right:* Former building of First Brethren Church of Philadelphia. While this photo was taken one hundred years later, you can still see the tracks where James drove his trolley each day.

Read: Acts 26:12-18

Reflect

It was 1904, and twenty-one-year-old James Gribble basked in his new-found freedom. Working as a streetcar conductor in Philadelphia was far less demanding than the farm he'd left behind in Mechanicsburg, and a steady paycheck gave him freedom to enjoy life in ways his friends at home only dreamed about.

That is, until the day tragedy struck. Hard. While the courts later cleared him of personal responsibility, for years James would carry the vivid images of the woman who was crushed to death while disembarking from the trolley he drove.

The accident occurred on a Saturday evening. Sunday morning, James sought help in a local church, finally willing to admit he needed God. Baptized that evening, on Monday he opened his Bible and discovered this verse: "Go into all the world and proclaim the gospel to the whole creation" (Mark 16:15). For James, the message was personal and unmistakable: *Go, James Gribble, and proclaim the Good News in Africa!*

Several years passed before James took pen in hand to reflect upon the importance of this moment: "Unless one gets a clear call from God in response to a definite surrender of one's will to Him, one had better not go to Africa. Many, many times in Africa, the fact that I was there by the will of God was a great and sustaining support to me. Candidates should make a clear and definite surrender of their wills unto Him whose right it is to rule their lives."

Concerning the type of person God calls, James observed, "Workers can be used upon the field with widely different degrees of qualifications. Truly we are living in an age when God is making manifest the abounding riches of His grace. We missionaries are full of spots and blemishes, yet God uses us to do the greatest work that has ever been committed unto angels or the children of men. It is said that Livingston was looked upon as an unpromising candidate for Africa."

What is the role of a *call* in determining who becomes a missionary? Opinions can differ strongly. On one side are those who assert that a call to missions is so intensely personal that no one should question it. On the other, there are those who completely dismiss the experience as too subjective to be useful. Looking for visible "evidence," they assert that a good testimony, appropriate training, and cross-cultural awareness are the best indicators of who will succeed in missions.

Yes, character, training, experience, gifting, perseverance, and flexibility are essential ingredients in confirming our fitness for cross-cultural ministry. But as any long-term missionary will tell us, when the going gets tough, what keeps us going is a deep conviction that God—personally and specifically—commanded *us* to go.

As a veteran missionary, James wrote these challenging words to a candidate who hoped to join him in Africa: "I would strongly recommend that you and yours learn to trust God to supply your need from day to day. . . . God is personally interested in your coming forth, else He had never called you. But if God has not called you, who has? Surely not the adversary. Therefore, having once been spoken to by God, let this suffice, and from that moment push ahead toward the goal which He Himself has set before you."

But will a firm conviction of our calling exempt us from obstacles? James continued, "Remember, a time of testing does not indicate in the least that God has failed you, but He may be searching to see if you will fail Him. Should you eat your last morsel, do not be afraid that God will forsake you. Many are the dear children of God who have had that experience. . . . My prayer and heart's desire is that you fail not. Faithful is He that calleth you, who will also do it."

Respond

For those who go:

1. Can you identify the specific moment when you sensed a clear and unmistakable *call* to missions? If so, what were the circumstances? What did you think? What did you feel? Who was the first person with whom you shared this experience?

2. What role did others fulfill in helping evaluate your readiness to deploy as a missionary? How did they affirm you? How did they challenge you to grow?

3. How might you explain how God leads men and women into missions to a young person currently seeking His will for their life? Can you identify someone today with whom you might share your ideas?

For those who send:

1. Take a moment to identify potential missionaries in your sphere of influence. What qualities do you see in their lives that lead you to believe God may be calling them into missions? Pray specifically for each person, asking God to grant them the ability to hear His voice and discern His calling.

2. Anyone taking first steps toward becoming a missionary will likely meet resistance arising from family members, health challenges, debt, or even social pressure from peers. What specific steps could you take today to encourage them as they seek to navigate these obstacles?

WALKING BY FAITH

NEW YORK CITY, OCTOBER 29–31, 1908

But seek first the kingdom of God and his righteousness,
and all these things will be added to you.

MATTHEW 6:33

Above: Setting sail on the *St. Paul*, October 31, 1908. *Right:* The ministry area targeted by the African Inland Mission is located in present-day Kenya. James later scouted new fields in Uganda and Tanzania.

Read: Matthew 6:25-34

Reflect

For a man accustomed to making his way in the world, the path to the mission field presented James with strange, new challenges. In his favor, he had a reputation for being disciplined, self-sufficient, and a good student, qualities which would serve him well as a pioneer missionary. Yet he lacked Bible and ministry training and needed time to mature in his newfound faith. Over the next four years, his local church became his school, and his pastor, his tutor.

But by 1908, James was growing restless. While glad his own

denomination was waking up to its responsibility to send missionaries, it was clear its energies would be consumed with sending a pioneer team to Argentina. So with the blessing of those who knew him best, James applied to serve with the Africa Inland Mission (AIM).

Early on, James learned to pray that God would mobilize others to give sacrificially to support his ministry, and one story stands out as a clear illustration of how God intended to answer his prayers. It was October 31, 1908, and James had just boarded a ship for Africa, carrying only enough money for passage to England. As the crew prepared to set sail, an elderly man hobbled toward the gangplank, crying out, "Is there a James Gribble onboard?" Minutes later, James was counting out $250 in English gold coin—more than sufficient to meet his immediate needs.

While the identity of this man remains a mystery, at least we know part of his story. During a prayer meeting the previous evening at his local church, he had been challenged to pray for the financial needs of James Gribble. Realizing that "faith without works is dead," he determined he would be the answer to his own prayers. But the ship was scheduled to sail at 10:00 the next morning!

By 9:00, the elderly gentleman was eagerly waiting in line at his bank. Emptying his savings account, he arrived at the dock only minutes before the ship was to set sail. For James, such a miraculous demonstration of God's grace "was more to him than the supply of his needs. It was God's seal upon his call and his ministry."

Like many agencies, AIM required its missionaries to raise financial support sufficient to cover their overseas expenses. This practice presents one of the biggest challenges to those considering missionary service today. We are products of a culture that deeply values independence and self-sufficiency. It goes against our nature to depend upon the generosity of others. Stated simply, it can feel like we're begging.

The first big step to changing this deep-seated cultural value is to ask a few simple questions: Have you ever considered how Jesus supported his ministry? How about Paul, Peter, and the other early missionaries? They gladly depended upon the generosity of others to supply their needs. Yes, since the beginning of missions, God has blessed some with the call to go and others with the responsibility to support them.

Jesus said, "It is more blessed to give than to receive." When missionaries invite others to support their ministries, they become windows of blessing into the minds and hearts of those who aren't called to go. Supporters of missions begin to think differently about the resources God entrusts them to manage. And they discover the *joy* of using those resources for what matters most.

Respond

For those who go:

1. For two thousand years, God has poured out blessings upon those who sacrifice by going. Can you identify some of these blessings in your own life? Take a moment to thank God for these blessings!

2. What are ways in which your attitudes toward raising support for missions may be influenced more by culture than by Scripture? Are these attitudes hindering God's freedom to work in your life? Could they be thwarting the work God desires to accomplish in the lives of those He's calling to support your ministry?

3. In light of your reflections, how might you better explain the privilege of developing a support base to a potential missionary?

For those who send:

1. For two thousand years, God has poured out blessings upon those who sacrifice by giving to support those who go. Can you identify some of these blessings in your own life? Take a moment to thank God for these blessings!

2. Have you ever asked God to increase your income so that you can increase your giving? How might this change the way you choose to save or spend? Is there an action step God is prompting you to take today?

SURVIVING CULTURE SHOCK

KIJABE (BRITISH EAST AFRICA), THE FIRST MONTHS FOLLOWING
ARRIVAL ON NOVEMBER 28, 1908

Abide in me, and I in you. As the branch cannot bear fruit by itself,
unless it abides in the vine, neither can you, unless you abide in me.

JOHN 15:4

Florence Newberry, James Gribble, and Mr. Hurlburt sailed together for British East
Africa (Kenya).

Read: John 15:1-8

Reflect

Setting sail on October 31, 1908, James spent the next twenty-nine
days traveling first to Europe, then through the Suez Canal down the
eastern coast of Africa, and finally via train to the mission station in
Kijabe. His traveling companions were Mr. Hurlburt, the director of
AIM, and Dr. Florence Newberry, another new recruit.

First settled as an outpost for evangelism among the Mukikuyu
tribe, Kijabe was well-situated near the Uganda Railroad, which provided missionaries access to telegraph and mail service. The higher

altitudes helped them avoid the constant swarms of malaria-bearing mosquitos that plagued those living in lower elevations. And it was an excellent location for creating a hospital and school, institutions that still serve the surrounding communities today.

Common to most new missionaries, James quickly discovered how little prepared he was for life in a radically different culture and climate. It's one thing to read and study about distant worlds; it's another to wake up one morning and realize this strange place needs to become *home*. With customary zeal, he threw himself into learning a new language and adapting to a new culture. Soon he was accepting assignments where his unique abilities were most needed: running the new sawmill and helping construct permanent houses for his coworkers.

As pioneer missionaries to Africa could purchase only basic food supplies in the local markets, everything else Westerners needed to survive such harsh conditions was either made by hand or shipped from faraway ports. James wrote, "We have no stove, but I intend to manufacture one out of bricks and sheet iron. Our food consists of bread, rice, milk and potatoes, both Irish and sweet. The latter when boiled in salt water with the skins on are delicious in spite of their being so stringy, having the flavor of bananas."

And like most missionaries, James was soon struggling with *culture shock*, that period of extreme disorientation that comes from a steady stream of new and strange experiences, usually lasting from six to eighteen months. One sure sign you're entering culture shock is when the "fun" and "exotic" experiences of tourism become the irritations and frustrations of daily life. Combined with increased spiritual opposition, culture shock often makes the first two years of deployment the most challenging of a missionary's career.

James observed, "Every missionary who goes to the field has great trials during the first year or so; sometimes for a much longer period. It is the attempt of the adversary to cripple the worker and make his failure as far reaching as possible. . . . What we need, as servants of God, is to exercise caution and be sure that we are walking in the will of the Lord. We need to be able to learn the mind of the Spirit, so as to render a verdict: 'It seemed good to the Holy Spirit and to us.'"

Some cross-cultural workers never really recuperate from culture shock. Others may learn survival techniques but allow a critical spirit to fester just beneath the surface. This spirit often appears during times of fellowship with other missionaries when we criticize the very people we're called to reach. If we're not careful, these negative attitudes become negative words and even negative actions toward nationals who seem to fail us.

How do we overcome culture shock? We must choose daily to abide in Jesus by allowing *His* love and *His* power to transform us into genuine agents of blessing to those *He* sent us to reach.

Respond

For those who go:

1. Think back upon your first years as a deployed missionary. What were some of the "seemingly little things" that frustrated you—perhaps out of proportion to their importance? Can you identify a moment or an event when you realized you had "turned the corner" so as to begin to gain victory over culture shock? What helped you reach that point?

2. Reflect for a few moments on the times of fellowship you currently share with other missionaries. What do you talk about? Do you focus primarily on frustrations or upon the unique blessing of living and working in another culture? How might the daily decision to "abide in Christ" help you?

3. Consider newly deployed missionaries who may be wrestling with culture shock. What tangible steps could you take today to encourage them to persevere?

For those who send:

1. New missionaries typically experience culture shock after six months and hopefully begin to overcome it by eighteen months in their new location. Make a list of missionaries in your sphere of influence who may be experiencing culture shock. Spend time asking God to grant them the ability to *remember why* they became missionaries and to *look beyond* their immediate circumstances.

2. What about the people who recently left homes in other parts of the world and now live near you? Have you ever paused to consider how they also experience culture shock? What specific action step might you take today to help them feel more at home in their new location?

LEARNING TO MANAGE DISTRACTIONS

AIM MISSION STATION, KIJABE, DURING 1909,
THE FIRST FULL YEAR ON THE FIELD

*No soldier gets entangled in civilian pursuits,
since his aim is to please the one who enlisted him.*

2 TIMOTHY 2:4

Left: James poses with his workshop. Note the string in his left hand as he takes an early selfie! Most of the photos in this book were taken by James. *Right:* A handy workman, James assisted with many construction projects, including this school building still in use today. The cornerstone was dedicated in 1910 by Theodore Roosevelt.

Read: 2 Timothy 2:1-13

Reflect

James Gribble was passionate about many things, including his favorite hobby: photography. He loved taking pictures, and Kijabe was a photographer's paradise. "I have been writing too many letters at night and spending too much time on photography," he wrote. "But I had to catch the mail, for the boats are sixteen days apart and my pictures are good ones."

Today, we're very grateful James enjoyed writing letters and taking pictures! Without those disciplines, we'd know little about his experiences in Africa and it would have been next to impossible to write this book.

But let's pause for a moment to look more closely at his words. Did you notice the important word *too*? He was writing *too* many letters. Spending *too* much time on photography.

This brings us to one of the most significant challenges faced by new missionaries: the temptation to allow the *good* and *better* to occupy the place we must reserve for the *best*. We're not referring to *evil* or even *questionable* practices, but the acceptable activities that soon become *distractions*, consuming time and diverting energy from the hard work of learning, adapting, and growing. Did Paul have this in mind when he wrote, "No soldier gets entangled in civilian pursuits, since his aim is to please the one who enlisted him" (2 Timothy 2:4)?

Today, some of our biggest distractions are the technologies which keep us tethered to those we left behind. With only a click or keystroke, we reconnect instantly with family, friends, and supporters in ways previous generations of missionaries could only dream about. But what seems a great blessing can quickly become a trap, limiting our capacity to build new relationships and postponing progress in adapting to our new world.

Writing and hobbies weren't James' only distractions. He frequently struggled with loneliness. And on more than one occasion, funds were so inadequate he would have fasted—involuntarily—if not invited to share a meal with a fellow missionary.

Bluntly stated, *missions isn't for the faint of heart!*

Yet in spite of these challenges, James could write: "I can truly say I am more thankful for my trials than my blessings. Oh, to be faithful unto the blessed Lord Jesus who left heaven's portals to die for me! Many lives have been laid down in Africa for Christ. Why not mine? Having put my hands to the plow, Oh, Lord, let me not look back.

May I always remember that if I suffer with Him, I shall also reign with Him. If it ever behooves me to lay down my life, may I die at the battlefront and not like a coward!"

Respond

For those who go:

1. Praise God that recent advances in technology provide us with many simple and inexpensive ways to stay connected with family, friends, and supporters. What guidelines have you and your teammates established so that this big blessing doesn't become a major distraction?

2. What advice would you give a new missionary seeking to maintain a healthy balance between work and hobbies, play and rest? Are there scriptural principles that support your ideas?

3. Missions is hard work, and James encourages us to be thankful for our trials. He also challenges us never to look back once we put our hands to the plow. Take a moment to meditate on today's Bible reading, asking God to renew within you a passion for staying focused on the attitudes and activities that best help you fulfill the mission He has assigned you.

For those who send:

1. Most missionaries will readily admit they face a daily struggle in their quest to discern between activities considered *good*, *better*, and *best*. Don't all of us face the same challenge? Ask God to work specifically in the lives of the missionaries in your sphere of influence, granting them the ability to discern the *best* activities to pursue today, while still maintaining a healthy balance between work and rest.

2. Have you ever paused to consider how the expectations you place on missionaries might become unintentional distractions in their daily lives? How might you foster good relationships while lowering the expectations they feel you are placing upon them?

ACHIEVING BALANCE BETWEEN "HERE" AND "THERE"

EXPLORATORY TRIP INTO GERMAN EAST AFRICA,
THE EARLY MONTHS OF 1910

I make it my ambition to preach the gospel, not where Christ has already been named, lest I build on someone else's foundation.

ROMANS 15:20

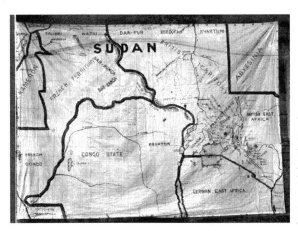

This early hand-drawn map (undated) may illustrate the lack of firsthand knowledge of the Kijabe Team with respect to "least-reached" territories to the west and south.

Read: Romans 15:14-21

Reflect

There was no question in anyone's mind that James Gribble was useful. The unique set of skills he brought to the mission station at Kijabe made life and ministry more tolerable for the entire missionary team. But he was also restless. While not denying there were great needs among the local population, his thoughts were drawn continuously inland, to regions with no knowledge of God and His Word.

Missiologist Ralph Winter divided the *Modern Era of Protestant*

Missions into three waves: ministry to the coastlands (1792–1910), to the interiors (1865–1980), and to unreached people groups (1934–??). As might be expected, the period of transition between each wave created a fertile breeding ground for misunderstandings among missionaries. Hardy pioneers launched each new wave at great personal sacrifice. They expected new arrivals to consolidate gains and develop the infrastructure for long-term ministry growth. Seldom did the pioneers feel it was time to move on and rarely were reinforcements content with staying put.

But didn't Jesus command us to penetrate *every* geographical region and make disciples among *every* people group? So why are we surprised when new generations of freshly minted laborers long to push beyond the territories their predecessors labored so hard to occupy?

Like the apostle Paul, James felt an inexplicable and constant draw to places where no missionary had gone before. With others who pursued "missions to the interiors," he could wholeheartedly agree with J. Oswald Sanders: "No one has the right to hear the Gospel twice while there is still someone who has not heard it once." Yet his teammates believed James and his skills were still needed at Kijabe. The work was still young and vulnerable, and they wanted to consolidate recent gains.

Refusing to be deterred, James tackled these objections with the strategy that always served him well—he went to his knees in prayer. "Once again, with renewed faith, I laid hold upon God in prayer— and told Him that I would go myself if He wanted me to and if He would make it possible. He then fully assured me that it was His will that I should go."

After lengthy discussions and much prayer, the team willingly released veteran John Stauffer and novice James Gribble to map out new regions for missionary work in the interior of Africa. The story of their adventures and trials rivals that of any pioneer in the modern era of Protestant missions. At one point, John fell so gravely ill

21

that he was forced to return to Kijabe for treatment. But James was determined to press on alone.

After claiming an entirely new region in German East Africa for his mission, James wrote, "I now have the official, written permission for Nera, and I have taken possession in the name of Jesus. I want to erect the buildings and get the general work started. Then I must leave and let someone else occupy. For my aim is to see the Gospel reach every tribe in the northwestern part of Africa. Many are the tribes waiting in darkness. Many are the millions who know not of Jesus. God forbid that I should cease to pray night and day for laborers. Oh, God, purge *me*, and send *me*, and put *me* always into the very thickest of the fight."

Respond

For those who go:

1. Have you experienced the age-old missionary tension between "consolidating gains" and "pioneering new fields?" What were the arguments offered in favor of each viewpoint? How might time spent reflecting on today's Scripture passage help guide such discussions in the future?

2. Before 1934, mission objectives were framed primarily in terms of geography. Now we frame them in terms of reached and unreached people groups. It's not an issue of "either/or" but "both/and." How might you explain this to the typical church member who helps support you?

3. As we move beyond the modern era of Protestant missions, we must ask, "What opportunities are being revealed by the Spirit of God that might define the *next* wave of missions?" Can you identify young workers who desire to be the pioneers of this next wave? (Are you one of them?) How might you help release these workers into new ministries?

For those who send:

1. Take a moment to consider your assumptions about missions. Were you aware that Jesus sends us across *geographical boundaries* (Acts 1:8) so as to reach *every people group* (Matthew 28:18-20)? How does this reality enhance your understanding of the Great Commission?

2. At the time of writing this book, missionaries were working in every *country* of the world. Yet there were still about seven thousand *people groups* with little or no gospel presence. Pray earnestly today that God raise up more workers to take the Good News to these people groups.

RENEWING VISION

CLAIMING NEW TERRITORY IN GERMAN EAST AFRICA,
THE FINAL MONTHS OF 1910

*Count it all joy, my brothers, when you meet trials of various kinds,
for you know that the testing of your faith produces steadfastness.*

JAMES 1:2-3

James interacts with members of the Agikuyu tribe,
part of a least-reached group first targeted by AIM near
Kijabe. A report seventeen years later spoke of hundreds
of converts and national evangelists.

Read: James 1:2-10

Reflect

Regional and local politics always impact mission work. In Africa,
policies that controlled the work of missionaries usually reflected
the agendas of exploitative colonial powers. In the case of German
East Africa, the colonists wanted to avoid the religious conflicts that
had kept Europe at war since the dawn of the Reformation. While
encouraging missionary activity, they insisted that only one religious

group work in each region. The first to arrive would enjoy exclusive rights to establish their mission program.

This policy helped compel James to press on alone into remote and unexplored regions of present-day Tanzania. After pitching his tent near Nera, about fifty-five miles south of Lake Victoria, he quickly set out to gain government permission to establish a mission station. Next, he focused on the grinding work of preparing adequate housing to receive reinforcements. Days passed quickly, consumed with surveying the land, building shelters, digging wells, and the myriad of other tasks required for expats to survive in such a harsh location.

It's likely that few missionaries have experienced isolation to the degree James suffered during those early days at Nera. Even busyness couldn't entirely blunt the pangs of loneliness. And to compound matters, he fell ill. Gravely ill. Hundreds of miles from the comforting words and helping hands of his teammates, James sweated and groaned with such a severe case of malaria that he despaired of life itself.

As often occurs when we reach the limits of our strength, God used this experience to bring clarity to James' missionary call: "Death is joyous to a believer, I know, and to depart and be with Christ is far better. For when I lay so ill at Nera on December 3rd, 1910, I seemed to be in the very presence of the Lord and though unspeakably joyous at the prospect of heaven, yet I watered my couch with tears for the lost. I saw pass before me then a panorama of the tribes of West Central Africa, and heard a voice speaking, 'Thou shalt be instrumental in carrying the Gospel to these.'

"Then I knew that I was not to die, but live. Then I knew that I had yet many a weary mile to walk for the Lord Jesus. It is exactly with me as though I had been raised from the dead for the evangelization of those very tribes. And now, day by day, I know not where my path may lead—but I will follow on. I would not dwell on this illness, but I can never be too glad for this experience which brought me into such blessed fellowship with the Lord, which taught me that my work was not yet completed, and in which I was given the never-to-be-forgotten vision of bringing the Gospel to many tribes who have not a missionary, not a soul to tell them of my Lord."

Respond

For those who go:

1. Thinking back on your journey as a missionary, can you identify a moment of crisis God used to either confirm or change the direction of your ministry? Have you paused recently to thank Him for intervening in your life?

2. How about the trials and challenges you are facing today? Can you identify specific ways God is at work to bring you to deeper levels of perseverance and maturity? And if His purposes are not yet clear, are you willing to take the faith step of thanking Him in spite of what you don't fully see or understand?

3. God used a severe illness to grant James a clearer vision about his future ministry, and he was forever grateful. How clear is your vision? Can you state it in twenty-five words or less? (Please don't be discouraged if you still lack clarity in this area. Persevere in prayer! As today's Scripture reading reminds us, we serve a God who delights in revealing His will to those who ask in faith!)

For those who send:

1. Ever wonder why God brings missionaries to mind, sometimes at what seem the most inopportune moments? Could it be that they are facing severe trials and need your help? Would you commit to interceding in prayer for these workers whenever God brings them to mind?

2. As Proverbs 3:5-6 reminds us, God's invitation to ask for wisdom shouldn't be limited to moments of testing and crisis. He delights in guiding His children with each step they take. Pause now to ask God to grant daily wisdom to the missionaries you care deeply about.

REVIEW

In this early photo, it's clear that the local population is adopting a "hostile posture." Are they opposing the efforts of early missionaries to share the Good News?

Today is your opportunity to review the Bible passages, reflections, and applications from the past week.

For those who go:

1. What is the primary spiritual lesson you feel God wants you to apply in order to reshape the way you think and serve as a missionary?

2. Is there a specific action step from your reading and reflection that you've postponed? Will you take it today?

For those who send:

1. What is the primary spiritual lesson you feel God wants you to apply in order to reshape the way you think and serve as a person who partners with missionaries?

2. Is there a specific action step from your reading and reflection that you've postponed? Will you take it today?

COUNTING THE COST

DIVIDING TIME AND ENERGY BETWEEN KIJABE AND NERA,
EARLY 1911 THROUGH LATE 1912

*Who is weak, and I am not weak? Who is made to fall,
and I am not indignant? If I must boast, I will boast
of the things that show my weakness.*

2 CORINTHIANS 11:29-30

James (center) with missionary team during his period of re-assignment. Meanwhile, Florence was released to join a pioneer team heading to Nera.

Read: 2 Corinthians 11:21-30

Reflect

Although alone, undernourished, and with threats against his life, James pressed forward with his labors at Nera. Convinced that reinforcements would soon arrive, he threw himself into building the mission station and evangelizing neighboring villages. But after months of intense labor, and to his great disappointment, he received word that someone else would soon replace him. James was needed to oversee construction projects at a new station not far from Kijabe. Would he return as quickly as possible?

A familiar tension faced by most missionaries is the constant pull between what we'd prefer to do and what our team or local circumstances most need us to do. With a heavy heart, James submitted to the will of his teammates and began the arduous journey back to the base camp. Funds were short, so he set out on foot, then booked third-class passage on a small steamer, and finally boarded the train to Kijabe.

As he settled into his new assignment, weeks soon turned into months. But James never forgot his dream to lead the charge into unevangelized fields. "When I get to heaven," he wrote, "and there see crowds of these bright faced people, perhaps I shall ask, 'Who are these?' And another shall reply, 'These are those who are rescued from dark heathendom in neglected Africa.' Oh, that He may be able to say—'through you.' What will trials, financial and personal, mean then? For I reckon that the sufferings of this present time are not worthy to be compared with the glory which shall be revealed in us."

With his assignments completed, James was finally released to join those already working in Nera. The small team of one couple, two women, and James poured themselves into completing the station and conducting evangelistic forays into neighboring villages. It was a season of exhausting work with little visible progress. After one unusually long day, James wrote, "Every bone and muscle in my body aches. This mountainous country with its narrow paths is altogether indescribable. To add to the difficulty, the long bamboo grass makes the jungle like a forest. As one tries to make his way through those narrow paths over which long grass has blown, one steps into holes, stumbles over stones, and utterly exhausted arrives at his destination too faint to eat. Most of the time I am a poor, weary old missionary who lives in a haystack. To make it worse I have so much trouble with my feet, but they are big enough to give any one trouble."

Yet somehow, James found joy in the midst of hardship. "I am inexpressibly glad that God permitted me to come to the foreign field. Had I a thousand lives to live, and the Lord wanted them all for use in Africa, He should have them every one. In spite of all my trials I would not trade my position for that of an angel in heaven. To help to rescue these perishing people is worth the life of any man. These tribes have never heard a single testimony for Jesus and have never had a single ray of Gospel light. I would rather go to Hell than to meet my Lord and not have done all that I could for these poor enslaved people.

"It is not the question of being able. It is a question of being willing. . . . If we love our Lord Jesus, shall we be afraid of the cost? He is not! I know that the Lord is faithful. His leadings are wonderful."

Respond

For those who go:

1. Take a moment to reflect upon a time when your personal preferences ran counter to the desires and plans of your teammates or mission leadership. How did you resolve this tension? If you had this moment to live over again, would you respond in the same way? Why or why not?

2. How might the decision to submit to the will of others enhance your ability to share the Good News with those God sent you to reach? Can you identify Scripture passages that support your conclusions?

3. The great inventor Thomas Edison is credited with observing, "Genius is one percent inspiration and ninety-nine percent perspiration." Even for those with a clear call to missions, sooner or later, the romance dims and we must commit to the discipline of everyday, hard work. Take a moment to ask the Spirit of God to grant you grace and perseverance to press on and to continue to "count the cost."

For those who send:

1. Sooner or later, every missionary will be called upon to choose between the needs and desires of teammates and their personal plans and preferences. Oftentimes it's not appropriate for them to share the details of these decisions with those outside their immediate team. Ask God to grant the missionaries in your sphere of influence the wisdom to balance personal preferences with their responsibilities toward others with whom they minister.

2. Take a moment to reflect upon your own struggle to balance the needs of others with your own preferences. Would you be willing to set aside a current project or ministry assignment for the good of the group? Why or why not? How might God desire to use the example of James Gribble to guide you toward making better choices in this area?

AFFIRMING SINGLENESS AND MARRIAGE

COURTSHIP AND MARRIAGE AT NERA,
JANUARY THROUGH AUGUST 1913

*Are you bound to a wife? Do not seek to be free. Are you free
from a wife? Do not seek a wife. . . . I say this for your own benefit,
not to lay any restraint upon you, but to promote good order and
to secure your undivided devotion to the Lord.*

1 CORINTHIANS 7:27, 35

James Gribble and Florence Newberry are wed in the heart of German East Africa,
August 12, 1913.

Read: 1 Corinthians 7:25-35

Reflect

Never prone to think much about the opposite sex, James was
entirely unprepared for the wave of emotions that swept over him

upon meeting Florence Newberry. Those feelings took root during the long passage from New York to Kijabe and only grew stronger as he watched how she threw herself unreservedly into her assignment as a missionary doctor. But James was both awkward and inexperienced in matters of the heart, so he resorted to what he knew best: He prayed fervently each day that God would work to awaken feelings for him in the heart of Florence.

As a potential suitor, his first challenge was how to get her alone long enough to declare his intentions. There was little privacy on the mission station, and, to further complicate matters, Florence kept a grueling schedule. So James settled upon a plan. Pretending to be ill, he would request an appointment with the young missionary doctor and declare his feelings for her. Finally, the moment arrived. But to his great disappointment, Florence patiently explained how she had pledged her heart to another who as yet did not share her call to missions. Would he promise never to pursue this topic again? Couldn't they just be friends?

Over the next few years, James worked up the courage several times to ask Florence to reconsider. Each time, she refused, fervently praying he would learn to love someone else! But by New Year's Eve, 1912, Florence was surprised to discover "that God was working in her heart a great and sudden miracle of human love."

Within days, they announced their engagement! Their teammates were not at all surprised.

"I am as sure that God chose my wife for me as I am that He called me to Africa," James wrote. "My strong leading to an implicit faith in God, my distinct call to the frontier make it imperative that I should have a wife, not for my personal happiness alone, but in order that I might be of the utmost value to God and to the work to which He has called me in Africa—and that she should have that same implicit faith, that same definite call."

He continued, "Frontier missionary life is so difficult that human love is not sufficient inspiration, nor can it furnish an enduring motive. A frontier missionary's wife must be willing to give Christ the pre-eminence in all things. She must be willing to make any sacrifice for the extension of the Gospel. Therefore, God must Himself reveal to the pioneer missionary His choice of a help-meet." And on a later occasion, he reflected, "No one should ever come to this field SIMPLY BECAUSE he or she is in love with another candidate. No missionary can successfully labor among these people without having a constraining love for their souls' salvation. Missionaries should marry only those who are missionary at heart."

Most everyone enjoys a story where girl rejects boy, he finally wins her love, and they live happily ever after. The slow-budding romance between James and Florence seems to fit this pattern. But let's take a few moments to reflect upon today's Scripture passage. In a world where many view singleness as *incompleteness*, Paul presents a very different point of view. The unmarried have a definite advantage over the rest of us, as they pursue without earthly distractions the mission of Jesus Christ. Throughout the ages, the story of missions among the least-reached is often the story of single women and men free to dedicate 100 percent of their focus, time, and energy for the cause of Christ.

Yes, we rejoice that God created a dynamic and balanced team in James and Florence, a team capable of holistic ministry to both body and soul. But let's never forget what they accomplished as single missionaries and what thousands of other singles have achieved through their undistracted dedication to the Great Commission.

Respond

For those who go:

1. While James appears to have "fallen head over heels in love" with Florence, he also recognized how both husband and wife must have a clear call from God if they are to succeed in

missions. How might you explain this reality to a young couple evaluating whether to deploy as missionaries?

2. Intentionally or otherwise, we often communicate that married life is *better* or at least more *complete* than life as a single person. Let's not forget that James and Florence married after serving five fruitful years as singles on the field. Reflecting upon today's Scripture passage, can you identify some tangible advantages of singleness in your field of service?

3. Take a moment to reflect upon single missionaries you know. Are there ways in which you and your team might unintentionally give the impression that they are incomplete? How might you better organize your team roles, relationships, and structures to ensure they are celebrated and treated as fully equal members of your team?

For those who send:

1. Take a moment to consider single men or women in your sphere of influence who are considering missions. How might the insights you've gained from today's readings inform the ways you seek to pray for them and encourage them?

2. Single missionaries aren't alone in facing the challenge of conflicting messages about their value and roles in the church. If you are single, what do you wish that married couples better understood about the unique opportunities and challenges you face as a follower of Jesus Christ? If you are married, how might today's readings challenge your attitudes and actions toward those God has appointed to be single? Whether single or married, would you be willing to take a positive step today toward fostering a healthy conversation on this topic in your church?

HARMONIZING DIVINE GUIDANCE WITH HUMAN COUNSEL

NERA, DURING THE FIRST MONTHS OF MARRIAGE,
SEPTEMBER THROUGH NOVEMBER 1913

*Where there is no guidance, a people falls,
but in an abundance of counselors there is safety.*

PROVERBS 11:14

The home James built for his bride. Covered outside with thatch and lined with tent canvas, it contained a kitchen, living room, bedroom, and storage area.

Read: Romans 8:26-30 and Proverbs 11:14

Reflect

James and Florence were married on August 12, 1913.

While true, that simple statement fails to capture the complications and frustrations of planning a wedding deep in the heart of Africa! The months had passed quickly since announcing their engagement, leaving barely enough time to order proper shoes and clothing, prepare the guest list, and plan the ceremony, all while working full-time in ministry. Increased activity at the mission station also attracted the attention of their "neighbors," and more than once they awoke to discover thieves making off with clothing and other supplies.

But the big day finally arrived. After a simple ceremony, friends gathered to celebrate a wedding breakfast. Then the happy couple walked the short distance to the home James had lovingly built for Florence. Covered outside by dried grasses and lined with tent canvas, it cost $8 to construct and contained a kitchen, living room, bedroom, and storeroom. Observing his masterpiece, the groom wryly commented, "People who live in glass houses must not throw stones. And people who live in grass houses must not build fires. But it is cold enough here now for anyone but an Eskimo."

Writing during their honeymoon, James provides a glimpse into their vision and their daily routine. "By God's help we hope to pave the way for the reaching of this entire tribe with the Gospel. Daily we spend two hours in prayer. We have from one to four native meetings daily and spend one day each week in the distant villages, my wife being carried."

Not long after the wedding, a letter arrived that would radically impact their future. Pastor Louis Bauman had played a key role in discipling James during his years as a young believer in Philadelphia, and, with Bauman's blessing, James had joined the Africa Inland Mission. But Bauman wasn't only a local pastor. He also served as a leader in the Foreign Mission Society of the Brethren Church. Having succeeded in opening Argentina as a mission field, the agency was ready to set its sights on a new field. "We feel that you must open for us," Bauman wrote, "in some untouched territory, a work which shall be distinctly of our own church and denomination."

How does a missionary discern when the time is ripe to begin a new chapter of ministry? What factors should she take into consideration? Or how does he make the big decision to leave one agency for another?

Today's Scripture readings point us toward two great sources of direction: prayer guided by the Holy Spirit and wisdom given through human counselors. Through persevering prayer and godly counsel, over time most decisions tend to become clear. In the meantime, we wait with confidence, as illustrated in this letter written by James to supporters in the USA: "Pray for us, that we may be so definitely led that we may make no mistake. I am glad that you think that I should be ordained. I am fully decided that I should be. I have been reading how God tried Hudson Taylor just before the China Inland Mission was organized. It has been a great help to me. I am so very happy that God led me to trust Him and to be a missionary. Louis S. Bauman and a layman named Harry Lingle were the ones used of God in leading me to trust Him. It is so blessed to trust the Lord. One never needs to be awake nights. Praise His Name."

Respond

For those who go:

1. Sometime after this episode, James wrote, "Let us remember that while on the Divine side true wisdom comes from Him alone, yet on the human side there is wisdom 'in the multitude of counselors.'" Reflecting back over your spiritual journey, what have you discovered about the dual roles of prayer and seeking counsel? How have you learned to balance the promptings of the Holy Spirit with the opportunity to seek input from others?

2. Is it possible that God delights in making His will more apparent to those with less spiritual maturity, while expecting the more spiritually mature to exercise greater faith and discernment by

waiting patiently upon God to know His will? Does this concept align with your experience? Why or why not?

3. James Gribble wrote, "It is so blessed to trust the Lord. One never needs to be awake nights." Are there decisions you currently face that are robbing you of sleep? Take time now to confess your worry to God, asking His Spirit to enable you to trust and wait until the answers are clear.

For those who send:

1. "Through persevering prayer and godly counsel, over time most decisions tend to become clear. In the meantime, we wait with confidence. . . ." What are you learning about persevering prayer and godly counsel in your own life? How might today's readings help you better navigate the journey toward understanding and embracing God's will for you?

2. Consider the missionaries in your sphere of influence. Whether or not you are aware of major decisions they are facing, intercede before God for each of them today. Ask Him to provide clear guidance through His Word, through specific answers to prayer, and through the good counsel of those closest to them.

SURVIVING SETBACKS AND DETOURS

FROM NERA TO CAPE TOWN, FROM DECEMBER 14, 1913,
THROUGH MOST OF 1914

What then shall we say to these things?
If God is for us, who can be against us?

ROMANS 8:31

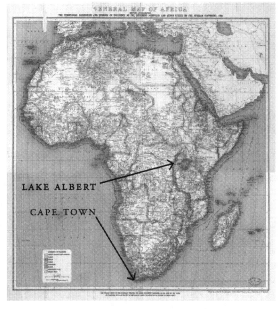

Dated 1909, this map helps illustrate both the European colonies and distances traversed by the Gribbles after Florence's illness. It would take almost a year for them to set sail from Cape Town to come to the USA.

Read: Romans 8:31-39

Reflect

While the newlyweds were still wrestling to discern God's will for their future, James and Florence welcomed the opportunity to set out on a three-week preaching expedition. After eleven days of intense ministry, they pitched their tent at a beautiful location on the shores of Lake Albert. It was Saturday evening, December 13, 1913, and they talked long into the night about their future ministry options. They hoped Sunday would provide time for rest and prayer.

But late that evening, Florence fell violently ill, and by morning she seemed near death. The closest hospital was more than two hundred miles away. As she suffered indescribable pain, James worked tirelessly over thirty days to carry her across difficult terrain by boat, porters, and train.

Upon arrival, Florence's worst suspicions were confirmed. She suffered from a ruptured appendix that had deteriorated into peritonitis. Without immediate surgery, the doctor informed them, at best she had one month to live. James wrestled in prayer as the doctors labored to save her life. For several weeks she hovered close to death. But by God's grace, her life was spared.

Over the next few months, as Florence gradually regained strength, James made himself useful by repairing and improving the hospital compound. Then came the fateful meeting with her doctor. While marveling how she had survived, he didn't mince words: "Take your wife home, and on no account ever bring her to the tropics again!"

It would be a year from when Florence fell ill before they could set sail for America. First, they had to make their way south over hundreds of miles to Cape Town, South Africa. Funds were short and the world was on the brink of war. On many occasions they enjoyed the hospitality of fellow missionaries. Yet there were times they were almost destitute, including a twenty-three day stretch when they were completely penniless!

"During these days," James wrote, "we have been taught many valuable lessons both in missionary and deputation work. The taking of high ground in our trials of faith, when we were tried as silver is tried, will be of inestimable value to us throughout our future service. Indeed I feel that we would fail in the work to which He is calling us did He not thus test us. But He has proven to us how faithful He can be to those who will trust Him in a foreign land. We continually praise Him for all His marvelous workings."

Always the student, James seized every opportunity to learn more about the politics, geography, and spiritual needs of central Africa. He remained convinced their present circumstances were only temporary setbacks. They would soon be redeployed to work in unreached regions.

"I am gaining much information which will be useful to us in the establishment of churches in Central Africa," he wrote. "I long to go to the darkest and most densely populated region, to a place where not only has the Gospel never been preached, but where no one else plans to preach it. In the vast section to which we hope to go, the influence of Islam is yet practically non-existent. What a barrier to its onward tread a line of stations across that beautiful country would be! That long grass country far beyond the bounds of civilization—how it beckons me on! The people are said to be agriculturists, hunters, and fishermen. They have no cattle, few sheep, and no fowls. They are said to be fierce cannibals, but that may be at least a partial exaggeration."

Respond
For those who go:

1. It is one thing to celebrate the goodness of God when our plans are prospering. It is another thing entirely to rejoice in His goodness when enduring intense trials with no clear light at the end of the tunnel. Reflecting upon today's Scripture passage, take a few moments to write down concrete reasons why we can *always* affirm the goodness of our God.

2. In the midst of "delays and detours," James observed, "I feel that we would fail in the work to which He is calling us did He not thus test us." Looking back over your personal experiences, how have moments of testing helped prepare you to be a more effective missionary?

3. Now consider your teammates. Is it possible that one or more of them are passing through an intense period of testing? What concrete steps might you take today to encourage them to persevere?

For those who send:

1. How did you respond to the obvious tension in today's reading between the doctor's prognosis ("Take your wife home . . .") and the optimism of James ("In the vast section to which we hope to go . . .")? In your opinion, was James exercising faith or was he presuming upon God? Perhaps it's impossible for us to know with certainty. As you consider the missionaries in your sphere of influence who face similar choices, pray that God will grant them the ability to clearly discern between faith and presumption.

2. The great missionary Paul wrote, "Who shall separate us from the love of Christ? Shall tribulation, or distress, or persecution, or famine, or nakedness, or danger, or sword" (Romans 8:35)? Attempt to rewrite Paul's list of trials by substituting the unique challenges faced by the missionaries you know. How does this enhance your prayer life for them?

MOBILIZING THE CHURCH IN AMERICA

DEPARTING CAPE TOWN, DECEMBER 3, 1914,
AND ARRIVING AT PHILADELPHIA, JANUARY 26, 1915

I rejoiced in the Lord greatly that now at length you have revived your
concern for me. You were indeed concerned for me,
but you had no opportunity.

PHILIPPIANS 4:10

Early "prayer card" photo taken after arrival in the USA

Read: Philippians 4:10-20

Reflect

It was a warm summer day in early December 1914. Armed with a
clearer understanding of the challenges of pioneer missions and fully
convinced they would soon return to Africa, James and Florence

finally boarded a steamer from Cape Town to England. After a short visit with missionary colleagues in London, they eagerly set sail for America, arriving in Philadelphia on January 26, 1915. The churches received them warmly, and soon they were outfitted with adequate clothing and supplies to face winter in the Northern Hemisphere.

Over the next three years, James and Florence would crisscross the continent in a continual, tireless quest to awaken interest for ministry in central Africa. Their message was simple: "The work is God's and not ours, and the most we can do for Him is just to yield ourselves up unreservedly to Him and let Him do with us as He sees fit. What a blessed thought it is that we can be used by the most high God. How willing we should be to let Him use us in any way; how glad that He never leaves us to our own devices."

They firmly believed there is a role in missions for *everyone*, expressed either through intercessory prayer and sacrificial giving or missionary service. With potential intercessors, they pointed to the example of Jesus: "Too much stress cannot be laid on Matthew 9:38, 'Pray earnestly to the Lord of the harvest to send out laborers into his harvest.'" Further, "The prayer bands will be the strong right arm of the African work. We want a series of such bands stretching from the Atlantic to the Pacific."

With potential donors, they issued the call to give sacrificially: "Faith must be exercised, not only by every true missionary but by every true donor. In other words, let not those who should give to a work refrain from doing so, thus saying, 'Let the ravens feed the Missionaries.' Let donors give largely, in obedience to the Great Commission. Let no acceptable volunteers be detained because the way is not financially clear for their support. We have the Master's promises. Only faith in them makes us capable of being witnesses for Omnipotence. However, the Great Commission applies to all who own Christ's name, and there should be a real entering into the work by those who remain at home."

With potential workers, they stressed how missions is both an *honor* and an *obligation*. "To preach the Gospel in Oubangui-Chari is a privilege angels would leave heaven to enter into—if only they had a chance." Further, James said, "My favorite theme is the Great Commission. Get Christian people to fully believe that the heathen apart from the Gospel are lost, and that we are the sole custodians of the Gospel, and there will be an awakening of interest in missions."

Then, as now, James and Florence encountered attitudes and beliefs that worked against their efforts to mobilize others to pray, give, and go. Perhaps the most insidious obstacle they faced was the unbiblical teaching that tribal peoples were exempt from suffering punishment for their sins because they were ignorant of God and His Word. "If ignorance could save the heathen," James retorted, "why should anyone be a missionary?" Using Ezekiel 33:1-6 to support his position, he continued, "The heathen are indeed being taken away in their iniquity. Without holiness no man shall see the Lord. But their blood shall be required of the watchman's hands. And the watchman is the church, whose duty it is to give the Gospel to the heathen."

These three simple challenges—to pray, give, and go—still form the rallying cry for cross-cultural missions today.

Respond

For those who go:

1. Throughout the history of the church, the enemy has worked hard to sow dangerous ideas that undermine both the *uniqueness* of the gospel message and the *urgency* with which we must proclaim it to everyone. Are some of those ideas taking root among those whom you are attempting to mobilize for the Great Commission? What Scripture passages might you use to refute those errors?

2. Mission mobilization can be summed up as providing concrete ways that others can *pray, give, send,* and *go.* In Philippians 4:15, Paul employs the word "partnership." How are you challenging those within your sphere of influence to join you as *partners* in one or more of these actions?

3. What specific action step can you take this week to better honor, thank, and encourage those who are partnering with you?

For those who send:

1. "My God will supply every need of yours according to his riches in glory in Christ Jesus" is a verse frequently quoted out of context. As a result, many fail to realize Paul wrote this promise to those who sacrificially give to support the work of missions. How should this new insight impact the way you understand and apply this promise in your sphere of influence?

2. In Philippians 4:15, Paul describes his relationship with the Philippian church as a "partnership." How would you describe the elements of a healthy partnership? What specific action could you take today to better fulfill your role as a partner in the Great Commission?

PREPARING TO GO (AGAIN!)

TRAVELING COAST-TO-COAST IN THE USA,
THE YEARS 1915 THROUGH 1918

*Trust in him at all times, O people; pour out your heart before him;
God is a refuge for us.*

PSALM 62:8

Marguerite was born to Florence and James on October 29, 1915. She was a source of great joy for both parents, but note James' awkwardness as he learns the joys of fatherhood. Marguerite would later marry Harold Dunning, with whom she spent many decades in fruitful ministry in the central region of Africa.

Read: Psalm 62:5-12

Reflect

Ever since his conversion, James had struggled with speaking in public. While seldom turning down an opportunity to preach, he was timid and frequently felt unable to meet the expectations others placed upon him. On one occasion, he wrote Florence, "Last night I gave my last lecture . . . on Mohammedanism, and was very dry. I was almost at my worst!" And on another, "I preached twice in

Cumberland on Sunday. Never did worse! But the Lord will not let His word return unto Him void!" And while he felt more competent in one-on-one encounters, there were times he let his emotions get the better of him. After one especially sharp encounter, he observed with chagrin, "I am a better soldier than a diplomat."

Anyone who has really seen the spiritual condition of our world and deeply felt compassion for the lost can sympathize with his frustrations. Fortunately, over time he learned to channel his feelings into prayers for revival among the churches he visited. As Florence observed, "When on fire for Christ, when filled with the Holy Spirit, then, and only then . . . would [the churches] be able and willing to furnish men and means to plant in other parts of Africa strong spiritual churches."

October 29, 1915 was a day of immense joy for James and Florence as they welcomed baby Marguerite into the world. Much like when he first met Florence, new emotions overwhelmed James as he experienced intense love for this precious gift while fumbling with awkwardness as he attempted to hold her. But the birth was hard on Florence. Still weakened by her frequent illnesses in Africa, she fell gravely ill and was hospitalized for three weeks. Months passed before she regained her strength. Once again, their future looked questionable.

"Our hope and trust is in God," James wrote. "Sometimes the darkest hour is just before the dawn. May we trust that it will be the case this time. He is Omnipotent, and He stands ready to use this Omnipotence for those who will trust Him. May we be given grace to trust Him now. It is always an easy thing to think that we trust God when everything is going smoothly, but at such a time as this we discover the actual strength of our faith and in whom it is placed. May God grant that our faith may be all in Him, that we may so trust Him that we may not disappoint Him. . . . Faith is nothing which we ourselves can produce. It is a gift, to receive which we need only be yielded to Him. 'Whatsoever is not of faith is sin.' May we press on to the highest degree of faith."

Always a man of action, James found the prolonged stay in America difficult. The first year passed tolerably enough, busy as they were with visits to churches and highlighted by the birth of their daughter. But much of the second year was consumed with Florence and her health challenges. As they entered their third year, the long wait became almost unbearable.

"We have been delayed in returning to Africa," James poured out his heart to a friend, "being in part hindered by the recent prolonged illness of my wife. Since this has been the case, may we be enabled to see in our disappointment, His appointment. His will be done. . . . We never felt more confident in his work than now, yet there are indeed mighty problems to be solved. But over every perplexity, every obstacle, by faith we can write, 'He is sufficient.'"

Twelve more months would pass before they finally set sail for Oubangui-Chari.

Respond

For those who go:

1. Like James and Florence, most of us have experienced the joys and frustrations of ministry in the homeland, taking great pleasure in time spent with family and friends while feeling frustrated at the lack of interest in missions we experience in many churches. How we long for them to see what we see and feel what we feel! Ultimately, James learned to channel his frustrations by praying for God to bring revival to the churches. What might God be saying to you through his example?

2. Consider the men and women you know who may currently be assigned to ministries in their homeland. Is there a specific way you could encourage them today?

3. Most missionaries are men and women of action. We'd much rather be doing something, *anything*, rather than waiting. Are you experiencing such a period now? Take a moment to review today's Scripture passage. How is God attempting to speak to you through this waiting period in your spiritual journey?

For those who send:

1. Over time, some missionaries who are effective in communicating in their adopted languages and cultures may become less effective in communicating when back home. Can you identify a specific way you might help them compensate for this challenge?

2. Think about those missionaries in your sphere of influence who must extend ministries in their homeland due to health, finances, or other circumstances beyond their control. Try to enter their world and sense what they might be feeling. Pray specifically today that God would grant them encouragement and strengthen their faith during this time of waiting.

REVIEW

James and Florence were convinced God was calling them
to pioneer missions work in the central region of Africa.
This photo illustrates some of the cultural chasms
they would be required to cross.

Today is your opportunity to review the Bible passages, reflections, and applications from the past week.

For those who go:

1. What is the primary spiritual lesson you feel God wants you to apply in order to reshape the way you *think* and *serve* as a missionary?

2. Is there a specific action step from your reading and reflection that you've postponed? Will you take it today?

For those who send:

1. What is the primary spiritual lesson you feel God wants you to apply in order to reshape the way you *think* and *serve* as a person who partners with missionaries?

2. Is there a specific action step from your reading and reflection that you've postponed? Will you take it today?

REFUSING TO COMPROMISE THE CALL

FROM NEW ORLEANS TO BRAZZAVILLE, JANUARY 8–MARCH 16, 1918

No one who puts his hand to the plow and
looks back is fit for the kingdom of God.

LUKE 9:62

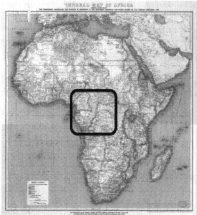

Left: Setting sail on the *City of Cairo*, January 8, 1918. From left to right, Estella Myers; James, Marguerite, and Florence Gribble; and Myrtle Mae Snyder. *Right:* While the target area for the pioneer party is located toward the center top of the square indicated, the only path forward was up the mighty Congo River and its tributaries.

Read: Luke 9:57-62

Reflect

Exhausted by a grueling schedule of visiting churches and making preparations for another term, the Gribbles were anxious to set sail for Africa. But the world was at war, and shipping lanes to Europe were far too dangerous to navigate. After much prayer, they determined their best option was to book passage on a ship heading down the coast of Brazil, then cross the South Atlantic to Cape Town. From there, a smaller steamer could take them up the western coast of Africa to the mouth of the mighty Congo River.

Estella Myers and Myrtle Mae Snyder made plans to join James, Florence, and little Marguerite. Both were trained nurses. The Gribbles came to know Estella through extensive correspondence while they still served at Nera. Myrtle Mae had just recently agreed to join the team, leaving her only six months to complete her preparations to live in Africa.

The first available ship was the *City of Athens*. But sensing no peace, James determined to wait. Within weeks came the news that it sank off the coast with great loss of life. The *City of Lahore* would sail next, but all berths were sold out. Later they learned it caught fire and burned off the coast of Brazil. The *City of Cairo* was the remaining option. After much prayer and soul-searching, the team of four adults and one child booked passage. Due to wartime conditions, they wouldn't know either the port or date of embarkation until just days before the ship weighed anchor.

"Things are going along nicely," James wrote, "but more slowly than I would like to see them. There is much more to be done, and there is only one way to do it. The more I do here, the less I will have to do in Africa and the freer I will be to do the work that we all go there to do."

Setting sail from New Orleans on January 8, 1918, the pioneer team was delighted to discover they sailed with fifty-four other missionaries, including a few that also hoped to penetrate the heart of Africa. The passage was uneventful and lasted only twenty-nine days, during which they made a valiant effort to learn Sango, the trade language of Oubangui-Chari, and French, which was spoken by regional officials.

They arrived at Cape Town on February 6, 1918. Within three days, they booked passage on the *Outeniqua*, a small steamer headed up the western coast to Luanda, Angola. From there, a smaller boat would navigate the mighty Congo River as far as Boma, in what today is the Republic of Congo. The *Wall* had no cabins, no railing, and no food service, and the journey would last thirty-six hours. Upon boarding, they immediately set about creating sleeping quarters on deck, preparing food, and tying a rope firmly around little Marguerite's waist!

An even smaller boat took them as far as Matadi, where they purchased tickets for the great Congo Railroad, a narrow-gauge railway that snaked some three hundred miles through the dense jungle to Kinshasa. From there they could easily pass over into Brazzaville. An amazing feat of engineering, the Congo Railway was carved out of the African bush over twenty years at the incredibly high cost of one European life per mile and one African life per yard of track.

"Bear in mind in your continued prayers," James wrote as they made their way to Brazzaville, "that we are about to enter one of the hardest fields in the entire world. Many of the tribes are reported to be cannibals. Mohammedanism will be continually besetting us. . . . Will you do all that you can to enlist prayer? We want to be wise as serpents and harmless as doves, and at the same time make no compromise with our calling."

Respond

For those who go:

1. In one of the most revered devotional books of all time, Thomas à Kempis wrote, "Man proposes, but God disposes" (*Homo proponit, sed Deus disponit*). Keeping in mind how God prevented the missionary team from booking passage on the *City of Athens* and the *City of Lahore*, take a few moments to reflect upon your own journey. Can you identify and celebrate incidents when your plans were thwarted only to discover God was intervening in your life?

2. In today's Scripture reading, Jesus challenges us to consider the cost of discipleship. Of the three men who figure in Luke 9:57-62, with which one do you most identify? Is Jesus calling you to recommit to the cost of following Him?

3. Think of how your own missionary journey might serve as an example to a younger or less experienced missionary. Would you consider reaching out to him or her today to share lessons you are learning about the cost of discipleship?

For those who send:

1. Take a moment to reflect upon the first question in the list above. Can you identify and celebrate incidents when your plans were thwarted only to discover God was intervening in your life?

2. Now take a moment to reflect upon the second question in the list above. How might Jesus be calling you to deeper levels of commitment in following Him? Is there a specific action step you sense He is indicating that you should take today?

ACCEPTING DELAY

*See how the farmer waits for the precious fruit of the earth,
being patient about it, until it receives the early
and the late rains. You also, be patient.*

JAMES 5:7-8

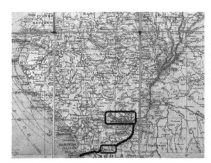 

Left: After sailing up the western coast of Africa to Luanda (Angola), the pioneer party boarded two smaller vessels that took them up the mighty Congo as far as Matadi, where they boarded the new Congo Railroad to Brazzaville. *Right:* Marguerite with her wagon and a giant African yam soon after settling in at Brazzaville. This picture helps remind us that the trials and obstacles faced by early pioneers impacted their children as well.

Read: James 5:7-11

Reflect

Within days of arriving at Brazzaville, James eagerly inquired whether permission had been granted to move further inland. Had the Governor-General received their letters of recommendation? Did he understand the purpose of their mission? Yes, he had reviewed letters sent earlier from America and their papers were in order. And yes, he now understood that they were volunteers and not, as he had assumed at first, trained from infancy as agents of the American church and government. But for now, they must wait. He must write to Paris to inquire whether special permission might be granted to allow them to establish a mission station in the Oubangui-Chari region. At least a thousand miles of river travel and two hundred miles by foot still lay between the pioneer missionaries and their goal.

As weeks turned into months, life gradually settled into a routine. The four adults busied themselves with language study, housekeeping, and the constant mending and repair their equipment required. Much of their flour and other foodstuffs were still at the docks in America, but the oatmeal and condensed milk would last for a time. They supplemented their diet with fish, chicken, sweet potatoes, beans, and other locally sourced products. But mostly, they waited. "Whatever may be the duration of our stay here," Gribble wrote, "the Spirit has not given us the liberty to turn aside elsewhere; we must tarry until the door be opened."

Housing proved an almost insurmountable challenge throughout their stay at Brazzaville. Every shelter they occupied either proved inadequate or was soon required by the owner for other uses. Often, they stayed in tents. From the fifth home they occupied during their first two months, James wrote, "In spite of our difficulties, we are not cast down but have been given a godly confidence, knowing that He is working and that governmental permission is sure. We know not how long we must wait, but we are absolutely certain that we shall not overstay His time, so we wait on in patience, counting it a privilege, and knowing those who are best at waiting are best at serving also." Further, he noted, "As to the future of the work, it is as bright as the promises of God."

But not all of the party shared James' optimism and willingness to wait. Always needing to be active, Myrtle Mae seized the opportunity to use her nursing skills with another mission in nearby Belgian Congo, abandoning the team after only three months at Brazzaville.

Lack of communication with the outside world only added to their trials, with no mail arriving until August, more than eight months after departing America. The remaining three adults were not idle, however, and among their more important achievements was the creation of the first English-Sango vocabulary.

"Our candidates should be those who can fully trust the Lord," James penned during these long months of waiting. "Those who can stand the test of being buried in obscurity and who are willing to live for Jesus under circumstances which may make life more difficult than death. . . . Let the work be sound in faith and doctrine, and let the workers know their God."

On another occasion, we can even sense a bit of irony in his words. "There are many worse places than Brazzaville. All of us would rather be here in obedience than elsewhere in disobedience. However, we will be greatly rejoiced when the path of obedience leads us into Oubangui-Chari."

Respond

For those who go:

1. Take a moment to consider the differences between assembling an automobile and planting crops on a farm. How are these tasks similar and how are they different? Why might *farming* be a good metaphor to explain the life of a missionary?

2. In today's Scripture passage we are exhorted to "consider those blessed who remained steadfast," and James cites the prophets and Job as examples. Can you identify three or four qualities in these examples that you would like to imitate in your own life?

3. How might you complete this sentence: *I can honestly thank God for times He caused me to wait, because through those experiences . . .*

For those who send:

1. Imagine that you were called upon to provide spiritual counsel for the members of this pioneer missionary team. As they faced uncertainty and delays, how might you use the metaphor of a patient farmer from today's Scripture passage to encourage them to persevere?

2. While it's unlikely you know many details about the day-to-day struggles of the missionaries in your sphere of influence, you can be certain that every one of them longs to see much spiritual fruit! Take time to pray specifically that each worker will follow the example of a good farmer by working diligently and waiting patiently for God to send an abundant harvest.

GETTING ALONG WITH TEAMMATES

THE LATER MONTHS IN BRAZZAVILLE,
FROM MARCH 16, 1918, TO SEPTEMBER 9, 1919

Who are you to pass judgment on the servant of another?
It is before his own master that he stands or falls. And he will be
upheld, for the Lord is able to make him stand.

ROMANS 14:4

Left: While the Rolliers had hoped to be part of the original team, various factors delayed their departure for almost a year. They arrived in Brazzaville on February 11, 1919. Note that Miss Snyder had already left the team. *Right:* Immediately after their house collapsed during a violent thunderstorm, the team took shelter once again in tents. The Rolliers stayed at the nearby Swedish Mission Station but spent their days with the team.

Read: Romans 14:1-12

Reflect

Born of French-speaking parents, Antoine Rollier grew up in Switzerland and immigrated to America at age twenty-one. His wife, Mary Ganshorn Rollier, was born in Russia to German parents, immigrating to America at age six. In 1915, at a prayer meeting in Long Beach, California, the Rolliers sat spellbound as James and Florence cast a vision for the proposed mission in Oubangui-Chari.

Within days, they volunteered to join the pioneer team, but health issues delayed their departure. Instead, they would become the first wave of reinforcements, arriving in Brazzaville in February 1919, eleven months after the early pioneers.

As a native speaker who also understood the idiosyncrasies of French culture, Antoine proved invaluable in navigating French bureaucracy. Mary was a nurse. Their daughters, Marie, aged eight, and Julia, aged five, provided the first playmates for Marguerite since the unfortunate death of another young missionary child some months earlier.

Warmly welcomed by the pioneer party, the Rolliers lodged at the nearby Swedish mission until suitable housing could be arranged. At this point, James, Florence, Estella, and Marguerite occupied a somewhat precarious house, once quite adequate for the tropics, but whose owner had long neglected its upkeep. It contained two rooms, one serving as a storeroom and the other as shared living space. The kitchen was outside. To take advantage of cooler nights, the adults slept in tents. The Rolliers joined them each day for prayer, work projects, and common meals.

But within hours of the Rolliers' arrival, a storm broke loose of such magnitude as was seldom seen in that region. Throughout the night, rain pounded against the walls, poured through the roof and washed across the floor. All were drenched except little Marguerite, who slept peacefully and stayed dry throughout the ordeal. But the team, their equipment, and their clothing were thoroughly soaked, and the house further weakened by the storm.

Within two weeks, the walls would collapse around them. The team had just finished dinner, and while they narrowly escaped serious physical injuries, the structure was damaged beyond repair. No other housing was available, so the team set to work building two small grass houses and rigging thatch awnings to protect their aging tents. To complete their new compound, they converted a bench into a makeshift table and two small boxes into cupboards, all with legs resting in cans of water to keep ants at bay.

Upon learning of candidates who showed interest in joining their team, James seized the opportunity to send some practical advice: Those considering marriage should first spend a year as singles on the field; single women missionaries are welcome and should be recruited; and "to be able to bear and forbear with others is necessary. . . . One usually manifests less grace on the mission field than at home."

Living under such stressful conditions certainly provided ample opportunity to witness the best and worst in each person's character. In a somewhat cryptic statement, James wrote, "Rest assured, if one is right and the other wrong, God will not permit that one to be continually wronged, but will sooner or later vindicate. God is faithful, and no one has a better right to experience every phase of His faithfulness than a foreign missionary.

"But it seems that upon entering these dark fields, one feels the darkness of his surroundings. And unless one sets himself at any cost, and by the grace of God, to have victory in his life, he will fail. Self must absolutely go under. Otherwise one's entire spiritual life is in jeopardy. As never before, we learn upon the mission field what it means to crucify self. It is only by the power of God that one is able to surmount the opposition of the adversary, who continually endeavors to crush us."

Respond

For those who go:

1. Regardless of whether there is actual research to support the claim, many believe the main reason missionaries leave the field is because of struggles with their teammates. Yet didn't Jesus called upon us to remove the log from our own eye before focusing on the speck in the eye of our brother (see Matthew 7:1-5)? In what concrete ways can you celebrate how living

cross-culturally has brought out the best in your character? And in what ways has it brought out the worst?

2. It's also been observed that missionaries tend to show greater patience toward nationals than toward their own teammates. Why do you think this occurs? How might the question, "Who are you to pass judgment on the servant of another?" help you develop greater patience toward those God appointed to work with you?

3. In today's Scripture passage, Paul exhorts us that "none of us lives to himself, and none of us dies to himself. For if we live, we live to the Lord, and if we die, we die to the Lord." How might you use this passage to counsel a younger missionary in her or his relationships to teammates?

For those who send:

1. Were you surprised with the candid statement, "to be able to bear and forbear with others is necessary. . . . One usually manifests less grace on the mission field than at home"? Why or why not? What factors might contribute to the special challenges faced by missionaries as they seek to live in harmony with their teammates? Pray today for *relational harmony* among the missionaries in your sphere of influence.

2. James' observation that "self must absolutely go under" is true for all followers of Christ, whether serving as missionaries or at home. Reflecting on your own spiritual journey, can you identify a relationship where God is calling you to honor another person above your own preferences and plans? What step will you take today to honor that person?

GROWING THROUGH WEAKNESS

ONBOARD THE STEAMSHIP *DJAH*, HEADING UP THE CONGO
AND SANGHA RIVERS, SEPTEMBER 9–26, 1919

*For the foolishness of God is wiser than men,
and the weakness of God is stronger than men.*

I CORINTHIANS 1:25

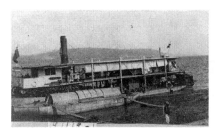 

Left: Heading up the mighty Congo River on the Steamship *Djah*, which offered only
two cabins with two berths each. James, Antoine, Estella, and little Julia slept on deck.
Right: The Sangha tributary would take them to north to Ouesso.

Read: 1 Corinthians 1:20-31

Reflect

"We praise God that at last the wait at Brazzaville has come to an
end," James wrote on September 12, 1919. "While we do not have
all that we have asked for and expect to receive, yet it is God in His
faithfulness who is leading us on. God is faithful, and when He tells
us to wait on Him we must wait, however foolish it may seem to do
so. Aside from the promises of eternal life for those who trust Jesus,
the promises to those who wait upon the Lord are the brightest in
the whole Bible."

While the eighteen months at Brazzaville had taken a toll on the
small missionary team, the trials of waiting were soon forgotten as

they prepared to steam northward to the government outpost in Carnot. Yet conditions would be cramped onboard the little steamship *Djah*, which offered only two cabins with two berths each. James, Antoine, Estella, and little Julia had to sleep on deck. But the change of scenery was most welcome, and all rejoiced they were finally making progress toward Oubangui-Chari.

Unfortunately, they were steaming through one of the unhealthiest stretches of the great Congo River. Weakened by the hardships of the past seven months and the constant strain of caring for her two daughters, who were often sick, Mary Rollier soon contracted an especially virulent strain of malaria. Over five days, as the boat continued its slow progress upriver, Mary's condition steadily deteriorated. On September 16, 1919, as she realized death was imminent, she turned her face toward heaven and gasped, "Only to do Thy will, O Lord." Her final words were, "I can see Jesus!"

Aged thirty-nine, wife and mother of two young girls, Mary Rollier was the first to lay down her life for the salvation of the Baya people of Oubangui-Chari. Lovingly placed in a hastily constructed pine coffin, she was buried later that day at the small government outpost at Ikelemba.

Within days of setting sail, Mary Rollier contracted malaria and passed away, the first casualty of many. She is buried at the government outpost in Ikelemba.

Pouring out his grief, James wrote in his journal, "Did ever a party so weak make an advance so desperate against strongholds so formidable?" "Only seven," Florence wrote of their group, "and three were children, two of them motherless, and the other not yet four years old! But God has chosen the weak things of the world to confound the mighty, and they went forward under the shadow of this mighty suffering, chastened by their bereavement and conscious that they might rest continually in the unchanging faithfulness of their God."

Back onboard, a smaller and much-sobered team determined they must press onward. Navigating their way up the Sangha River to the village of Ouesso, located at the northernmost tip of present-day Republic of Congo, they paused to rest for three days. Then they boarded the *Ngandou*, an even smaller steamer, for the four-day trip to Nola, arriving on September 26, 1919.

"We more and more realize," James wrote from Nola, "that the making of Christ known in the French Soudan is not going to be an easy task. It is only by a strong faith in God that the work will be done. . . . Just this morning I read in the Word the following: 'His Divine Power has granted to us all things that pertain to life and godliness' (2 Peter 1:3), and I am convinced that this comprises all the supply that a missionary needs to fulfill the mission on which God has sent him."

Respond

For those who go:

1. Over the past two thousand years, the story of the Great Commission has been the story of unassuming men and women who in weakness have stepped out in faith against often insurmountable odds. From a human perspective, their efforts appeared certain to fail. And if measured in terms of sicknesses and setbacks, those efforts have often "failed." Yet in today's passage, the great missionary Paul reminds us that "the

foolishness of God is wiser than men, and the weakness of God is stronger than men." Reflecting on your personal journey, can you celebrate moments when your life illustrated this truth?

2. Now take your thoughts and turn them into praise, following the admonition of Paul who also said, "Let the one who boasts, boast in the Lord."

3. In spite of overwhelmingly difficult circumstances, James found encouragement in the words of Peter, another great missionary, who observed, "His divine power has granted to us all things that pertain to life and godliness . . . by which he has granted to us his precious and very great promises." Why not write one of those promises on a card and place it in a prominent place where it will remind you throughout the day of God's faithfulness?

For those who send:

1. Take a moment to reflect upon the first question in the list above. Reflecting over your personal journey, can you celebrate moments when your life illustrated this truth?

2. Now consider the missionaries in your sphere of influence. Spend time praying this prayer for each of them, adapted from 2 Peter 1:3-4:

> Lord God, I intercede for [insert name], asking that at this very moment You give them a fresh understanding of all they are granted in Christ, including life, godliness, knowledge, and a fuller understanding of Your great and precious promises.

PURSUING THE FULLNESS OF THE SPIRIT

THE SIX-WEEK DELAY AT NOLA,
SEPTEMBER 26 TO NOVEMBER 10, 1919

*Those who belong to Christ Jesus have crucified the flesh
with its passions and desires. If we live by the Spirit,
let us also keep in step with the Spirit.*

GALATIANS 5:24-25

The pioneer team was warmly welcomed in Nola, where the French official strongly
urged them to take up permanent residence. Even tribal leaders like Chief Dajou
attempted to influence the missionaries, bringing many of his eighteen wives for them to
meet. Later they posed for another photo with their "celebration clothing." See Florence
and Estella at the back.

Read: Galatians 5:16-26

Reflect

The pioneer team was only hours from arriving at Nola when they
discovered an unfortunate mistake in their passports. Someone
had written "Nola" instead of "Carnot." They would be detained
until letters could be sent to correct the error. But would they consider making Nola their home, the government official inquired? A
medical center staffed by Westerners, he reasoned, would signifi-
cantly enhance the quality of his outpost.

The French official worked hard over the next six weeks to make their stay comfortable, providing two attractive houses which certainly ranked among the most comfortable they had enjoyed since entering Africa. Yet while pleasing to the eye, the homes were poorly located near the convergence of two rivers and held captive by swarms of tsetse flies. Every team member suffered from low-grade fevers. They would gladly continue the journey upriver as soon as permission was granted.

But all things considered, it was good to be off the crowded steamer, and the pioneer team was determined to take full advantage of the opportunity to practice language skills and study local customs. This was their first real opportunity to be face-to-face with the Baya, members of the very cluster of tribes for whom they had prayed and traveled so far to share the Good News. As was to be expected, the three American girls attracted lots of attention and opened many doors. And their little bicycle and wagon, carried so carefully over so many miles, proved another irresistible attraction to the surrounding population.

Among the heavy correspondence and journal entries James recorded during the stay in Nola, we gain a glimpse into his understanding of the indispensable role of the Holy Spirit in missions. Here are some excerpts, published later by Florence:

"In order to prove to the world once more that the Gospel of Jesus Christ has not lost its power to change men's lives, we need more than the ability to preach the Gospel well in the native language, for the natural heart is unwilling to be reconciled to God. . . .

"No amount of missionary machinery will solve the problem. Nothing but the mighty working of the Holy Spirit in the people among whom we preach will bring the desired results. That is the issue; we absolutely must have an outpouring of God's Holy Spirit upon the people themselves. Nothing else will do. And we must not be deceived into thinking that anything else will do. Schools and medical work will serve to get us into closer touch with the people, but they have in themselves no power to transform the heart.

"But the Holy Spirit cannot work among a native people except as He goes out through our lives as missionaries. We must not only have the gift of the Spirit, which is the heritage of all believers, but we must be actually Spirit-filled. The Holy Spirit must take hold of our lives and control them absolutely.

"Pray that we may be kept free from all sin and selfishness, so that the Holy Spirit may have the right-of-way in our lives. Along this very line missionaries need your prayers most. We do need your prayers that our bodies may be kept strong, but a thousand times more do we need them that we may constantly be filled with the Holy Spirit, for it is only then that we can fully reveal the Lord Jesus. It is almost useless to pray for a mighty working in the hearts of the natives if the Holy Spirit has not complete control in the lives of the missionaries.

"Therefore, in the interest of the entrance of the Gospel into the Eastern French Sudan, we earnestly plead with you for prayer for a mighty outpouring of the Holy Spirit here, BEGINNING WITH THE MISSIONARIES."

Respond

For those who go:

1. Reflect upon moments in your journey as a missionary when you most sensed the Holy Spirit at work among those you were seeking to reach. What made this experience unique? Can you identify factors in your life that permitted the Spirit to work freely through you?

2. In today's Scripture reading, Paul challenges us with this thought: "If we live by the Spirit, let us also keep in step with the Spirit." How would you complete this sentence? *I know I am "keeping in step with the Spirit" when . . .*

3. Now take time to talk with the Holy Spirit through prayer. Ask how you might better reflect your dependency upon Him in your ministry to others. Then ask Him to show you ways in which He desires to have *more control* over your life today.

For those who send:

1. "No amount of missionary machinery will solve the problem" was James' way of pointing out how the *activity of missions* should never be confused with the *power for missions*. He listed schools and medical facilities as examples of those activities in his ministry context. What are the most common *activities* among missionaries in your sphere of influence today? Based upon today's readings, how might you encourage missionaries to remember that the true *power* for missions is found only in the Holy Spirit?

2. James also urged the folks in his homeland to pray continually for a mighty outpouring of the Holy Spirit, beginning in the lives of missionaries. Take time to pray this same prayer for missionaries in your sphere of influence.

FIXING OUR EYES ON THE ULTIMATE PRIZE

TRAVELING BY CONVERTED WHALEBOATS AND BY FOOT,
FROM NOLA TO CARNOT, NOVEMBER 10–24, 1919

Worthy are you to take the scroll and to open its seals, for you were slain, and by your blood you ransomed people for God from every tribe and language and people and nation.

REVELATION 5:9

Left: From Nola, the pioneer team boarded converted whaleboats, which they outfitted with straw coverings for protection from the merciless sun. *Right:* Equipment was loaded either on smaller boats or this large canoe, carved from a single tree and capable of carrying up to seven tons of cargo.

Read: Revelation 5:6-14

Reflect

Now that they had finally met and conversed with the Baya, the missionary team was even more anxious to press on toward Oubangui-Chari. They were making good progress in writing English-Sango and French-Sango grammars and dictionaries and were growing more fluent in conversational Sango. To the deep regret of both the French and native inhabitants of Nola, it was time to press on.

Writing shortly before their departure, James observed, "Satan will not permit us to make the Name of Jesus known in this dark land without contesting every inch, but it is by faith that we shall win; and we shall meet many redeemed ones from the Baya, and possibly many other tribes, in glory when our work on earth, till He come, is done."

Navigating the Mambere River from Nola to Carnot required a new form of transportation. Years before, some ingenious trader had managed to import small, steel boats formerly used in whaling operations. James hired two of these sturdy crafts to carry the missionaries and a portion of their provisions. But before they could set sail, they had to rig small grass shelters in the center of each boat as a shield from the blistering rays of the sun. For the remaining equipment they hired a large canoe, hollowed from a single tree and capable of carrying seven tons of cargo.

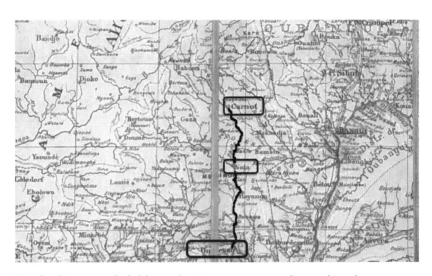

Traveling by converted whaleboats, the pioneer team averaged one mile per hour, camping on the shore each evening. At Bania, they forded the falls on foot.

Setting out from Nola on November 10, 1919, at an average speed of one mile per hour, they began the five-day journey north to

Bania. Ten native oarsmen were assigned to each boat with instructions to stay close to the shore to avoid the swift current and occasional whirlpools. After spending ten to twelve hours on the river, most evenings they camped on the shore, cooking over open fires and nesting down as best they could to keep warm. Temperatures often dropped precipitously at night. The children were urged to remain close and quiet, as rumors circulated of leopards running freely in the nearby bush.

After a brief rest in Bania, they set out on foot to Ikaya. This seven-mile walk occupied a full day and allowed them to skirt the treacherous falls. But turbulent waters weren't their only concern. "The further we go, the fiercer becomes the opposition," James wrote, "but thanks be unto God, they who are for us are more than they that be against us."

After hiring other converted whaleboats at Ikaya, for six more days the pioneer team continued upriver at much the same pace. Food was scarce during the entire journey and little Marguerite suffered both frights and fevers. On one occasion, as the native oarsmen pulled up to the shoreline to rest, she was startled to tears by the harsh cry of a young boy she considered a friend. But he was only attempting to save her life, having spotted a leopard ready to pounce from a tree limb not far above her head.

Exhausted from their ordeals, the missionary party finally arrived in Carnot. It was November 24, 1919, three months since they had departed Brazzaville. They were warmly received and soon were feasting at the table of a local French official. But once again, adequate housing was scarce. Fortunately, a generous member of the Forestry Company offered the temporary loan of a house. Its three rooms would serve as bedrooms, and they could eat and live on the veranda.

The second year in Africa was drawing to a close. Through many trials and detours, God had always proven faithful. Little did the team realize they were about to enter their most trying year yet.

Respond

For those who go:

1. For almost two thousand years, those committed to making disciples among unreached people groups have been greatly encouraged by Revelation 5:9: "By your blood you ransomed people for God from every tribe and language and people and nation." In spite of the obstacles we encounter, the outcome is guaranteed! There will be a harvest of souls from every linguistic and ethnic group! Take a moment to imagine the faces of those whom you are working hard to reach. Can you envision a day when you will stand together before the throne of God? How does that give you the courage and motivation to press on?

2. James observed, "Satan will not permit us to make the Name of Jesus known in this dark land without contesting every inch, but it is by faith that we shall win." Contrary to popular ideas, biblical faith is not simply a strong wish or desire that something happen. Rather, it is *choosing to believe* God will fulfill His promises and *acting upon that belief.* List two or three promises from the Bible that apply to your specific situation. How might you choose to act upon those promises today?

3. Take a few moments to praise God for always, always, *always* being true to His promises!

For those who send:

1. What do you know about the specific disciple-making focus of missionaries in your sphere of influence? Can you identify these people by their tribe, language, politics, or ethnic group? How might a better understanding of the uniqueness of each group help you better appreciate the unique ministry of each missionary?

2. Revelation 5:9 illustrates that no matter how we divide up our world—by tribes or languages or politics or ethnic groups— each group will one day be represented in heaven! Could there be any greater encouragement for those who care about missions? Take a moment to praise God for the fruit that will one day be gathered from every group where your missionaries are at work!

REVIEW

Taken near Nola, this photo features men of the Kande tribe.

Today is your opportunity to review the Bible passages, reflections, and applications from the past week.

For those who go:

1. What is the primary spiritual lesson you feel God wants you to apply in order to reshape the way you think and serve as a missionary?

2. Is there a specific action step from your reading and reflection that you've postponed? Will you take it today?

For those who send:

1. What is the primary spiritual lesson you feel God wants you to apply in order to reshape the way you think and serve as a person who partners with missionaries?

2. Is there a specific action step from your reading and reflection that you've postponed? Will you take it today?

SUFFERING YET PERSEVERING

THE FIRST MONTHS IN CARNOT,
INCLUDING LATE NOVEMBER 1919 AND EARLY 1920

And all these, though commended through their faith, did not receive
what was promised, since God had provided something better for us,
that apart from us they should not be made perfect.

HEBREWS 11:39-40

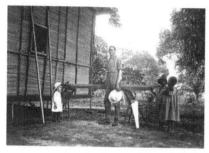 

Lack of adequate housing continued to be a serious problem during the eighteen months the team spent in Carnot. These photos show the industry of James, who built a structure to keep out moisture and leopards (see Day 23).

Read: Hebrews 11:32-40

Reflect

Although Oubangui-Chari was located only a hundred miles due north of Carnot, for the trials that lay ahead, it could have been an ocean away. "No one should think of coming here," James penned, "who is not prepared to suffer hardships such as he never dreamed of. The battle is hard. We are subjected to the fiercest fire of the adversary. But God is faithful, and all that we need to be cautious about is to be found abiding in Him."

As is often the case, the most significant battles were raging within. Were these trials and delays God's way of informing them they had mistaken His will, or was He calling upon them to persevere? In the midst of such soul-searching, only one thing is certain: God will never abandon us. "Even though we may have erred," James reflected after one especially intense period of soul-searching, "God will undertake for us. In His faithfulness He has not and will not forsake us."

And many were the trials from without. The first major crisis was an inability to cash checks. Yes, there were sufficient funds in their bank accounts. They simply couldn't access them. Checks were typically refused at Carnot on some minor technicality, and it could take up to two months to correct the problem. Their perpetual shortage of funds often prevented them from purchasing food and finding adequate housing. "Never since 1914 have we been so low financially," James wrote, somewhat tongue-in-cheek. "Unless our funds soon reach us in cashable form, we will have wonderful stories to relate of God's REMARKABLE PROVISION when the USUAL supply fails."

As in Brazzaville, housing options were quite limited. After three months in the small house loaned by the Forestry Service, they were informed it was needed for other purposes. What's more, the rainy season was fast approaching and credible stories were circulating of a man-eating leopard on the loose. Their only recourse was to clear the brush from a vacant lot, pitch their tents in a circle, and keep a large fire blazing throughout the night.

Educating and entertaining the three children presented another challenge, made more complicated because they believed it necessary to keep them indoors from 10:00 a.m. to 4:00 p.m. to avoid the worst disease-bearing insects. Mail arrived infrequently and many packages were lost in transit. To add to these trials, there was a severe shortage of kerosene and candles throughout the region. Often the team was forced to burn sesame oil in crude lanterns or spend their evenings in total darkness.

Such trials might overwhelm a physically and emotionally healthy individual, but seldom were they completely healthy. Due to sunstroke, Antoine suffered severe migraines. His daughters were frequently ill with fevers that could last several weeks. On one frightful occasion, Marguerite's temperature spiked six degrees in just forty-five minutes. And James, Florence, and Estella weren't exempt from sudden and prolonged illnesses. Hardly a day passed when someone didn't require active nursing care.

"Here we have encountered terrific opposition," James wrote. "The adversary has seemingly marshalled all his hosts against us. Except that God will undertake mightily for us, our situation would indeed be hopeless."

Like others before them who faced the limits of their emotional and physical endurance, the small team responded with the only resource at their disposal. They prayed. To paraphrase James' words, "Except when interrupted by moving, building, illnesses, etc., each day we spend from 9:00 to 11:00 a.m., from 2:00 to 3:30 p.m., and evenings in earnest prayer that the Gospel go forth in this land. In these seasons of prayer, we are given much assurance by the Lord that He who hath been faithful will yet be faithful, and our part is that of waiting on Him in prayer until He does the work."

Respond

For those who go:

1. The first section of Hebrews 11 recounts the amazing stories of men and women who trusted God and came out victorious. But for today's reading, we selected the lesser known final paragraphs. They highlight the countless and nameless servants of God who suffered without seeing the outcome of their faith. With which set of stories do you most identify today? Why?

2. What every story from Hebrews 11 shares in common is how God is honored through persevering faith. Take a moment to consider past lessons God taught you about persevering through periods of sickness, shortages, and delays. Will you allow those lessons to encourage your faith today?

3. Is it possible that some of your fellow workers are facing intense trials and are "suffering in silence?" How might you reach out to them to encourage them to persevere?

For those who send:

1. Modern technology makes it possible for us to maintain frequent contact with missionaries. On the positive side, this creates opportunities for us to "bear one another's burdens" (Galatians 6:2). But have you considered that too much instant communication might have a negative side, as "each will have to bear his own load?" (Galatians 6:5). Moving too quickly to alleviate a stress or meet a need might cause us to unintentionally short-circuit the work God desires to accomplish in the mind and heart of a missionary. The solution? Before rushing to meet a need, pray for much wisdom and be willing to consult with others who may be in a better position to understand the situation.

2. In spite of great pressures on their schedule, James and his missionary teammates determined that prayer was more than simply "a way to start the work." They believed that prayer *is* the work and built their schedules around regular seasons of prayer. What do you learn from their example that inspires you to plan prayer into your daily schedule?

ENGAGING IN SPIRITUAL WARFARE

ALSO THE FIRST MONTHS IN CARNOT,
INCLUDING LATE NOVEMBER 1919 AND EARLY 1920

*For we do not wrestle against flesh and blood, but against the rulers,
against the authorities, against the cosmic powers over this present
darkness, against the spiritual forces of evil in the heavenly places.*

EPHESIANS 6:12

Left: An African receives medical care from the missionary team after being attacked by
a man-eating leopard. *Right:* The village (and missionaries) breathed a great sigh of relief
when the leopard was finally trapped and killed.

Read: Ephesians 6:10-20

Reflect

The threat of attack from wild animals was nothing new to James and
Florence. They had dealt with this reality years earlier in German East
Africa and later while working their way upriver toward Oubangui-
Chari. But at Carnot, they discovered something new. During the
Great War of 1914–1918, German and French troops engaged in
a bloody and prolonged struggle for supremacy in the region. The
wounded and dead they abandoned on the battlefields were easy
prey for animals formerly unaccustomed to human flesh. With this

new taste for human blood, gorillas and leopards now preyed upon unsuspecting villagers. One particular leopard stalked Carnot as his favorite hunting grounds.

The missionary team learned of this danger while still living at the house loaned by the Forestry Company. Unaccustomed to running from danger, James continued his habit of sleeping on the veranda, with only a thin mosquito net to protect him. That was destined to change, however, when he was awakened one night by a sharp cry. The leopard was making off with the night watchman, and his young son was screaming for help. Frightened by the noise, the leopard abandoned his prey and slipped quietly into the dense underbrush. Though he was bleeding from the head and badly shaken, the watchman would survive after receiving prompt medical care from Florence and Estella.

Over the next few weeks the leopard continued to stalk the village. Concerned for the safety of the Americans, the local French official soon sent his troops to help construct a safer dwelling. Yet even in their new home, they lay awake many nights with the sounds of the leopard scratching against the barred windows and doors. Finally, the leopard itself became prey, captured in an ingenious trap and killed by local soldiers.

But the story has a significant spiritual twist, which James attempted to explain to his supporters in America. "A man who consents to become a human leopard has the direction of a leopard in the bush. He exerts sufficient power over the beast to control his movements, causing him to visit those whom the man wishes to annoy. This power is, of course, Satanic. Many pay him for his protection from the leopard. When a man, however, consents to receive this diabolical power, he covenants with the devil to die simultaneously with the leopard. The night this leopard was killed, his human control [demon-possession] died in a village not far from Carnot.

An official formerly here found that imprisoning the witch doctors lessened leopard depredations."

"To you," he continued, "the above must seem like an idle story, but it is not so with us. The more one comes in contact with heathenism, the more one realizes the actuality of the diabolic supernatural powers of darkness. . . . God only knows what powers we have to combat in bringing the Gospel to the inhabitants of this dark land. But He is for us! Who can be against us?"

The first reaction of many in the Western world is to dismiss such ideas as mere superstition, choosing to believe only in a world that can be seen, touched, measured, and analyzed. But both the Scriptures and the testimonies of missionaries inform us of an unseen world every bit as real. These two worlds are in constant, dynamic tension, and to ignore the spiritual world is to place at peril the very people we want to reach.

The pioneer missionary team was locked in an intense battle for Oubangui-Chari which raged on both spiritual and physical fronts. Not long after the experience with the leopard and while convalescing from yet another prolonged illness, James wrote, "We are still holding by His grace the fort here at Carnot. We know that He who hath called us is faithful. However, the battle is increasingly hard and we feel opposition on every hand. Satan never opposed us more vigorously."

Respond

For those who go:

1. What are you discovering about the "unseen world" in your field of ministry? Can you identify specific ways in which Satan and his forces are influencing the "seen" world? How?

2. "Fight or flight" seems to describe the polar opposite ways many believers respond to Satan's influences. In contrast, Paul

instructs us to "put on the whole armor of God, that you may be able to *stand* against the schemes of the devil" (Ephesians 6:11, emphasis added). What does this look like for you in your context?

3. Perhaps you feel inadequately prepared to understand and appropriately engage the spiritual warfare that rages around you. With whom might you discuss "spiritual" or "unseen realities" this week? Will you reach out to this person today?

For those who send:

1. Writing over one hundred years ago, James was convinced that few people in his homeland would agree with his firm conviction that a leopard could be controlled by demonic powers. How about you? Is there anything about today's reading you find difficult to believe? Do you know a missionary or a qualified pastor who might be willing to teach you more about "the powers of the unseen world?" Why not reach out to this person today?

2. Focus your prayers today on the need for missionaries in your sphere of influence to "put on the whole armor of God, that [they] may be able to stand against the schemes of the devil" (Ephesians 6:11). From whatever angle those spiritual attacks may come, ask God to grant strength and courage to resist through the spiritual armor He supplies.

LOSING TEAMMATES

THE LATER MONTHS IN CARNOT,
FROM THE MIDDLE OF 1920 THROUGH JANUARY 1921

*For the moment all discipline seems painful rather than pleasant,
but later it yields the peaceful fruit of righteousness
to those who have been trained by it.*

HEBREWS 12:11

Left: Myrtle Mae Snyder, one of the original pioneers, contracted malaria and died before rejoining the team. *Above:* Earlier months in Brazzaville represented happier days for the Rollier family. Still grieving the loss of their wife and mother, Antoine and the two girls returned to the USA shortly after the death of Miss Snyder.

Read: Hebrews 12:1-11

Reflect

"I have no idea how the Lord will bring about our entrance into definite missionary work," James wrote as the stay at Carnot extended into the latter half of 1920, "yet I know that it will come. It is our business to stand fast in the Lord, waiting upon Him to make it

91

possible for us to enter into the work to which He has called us. The battle is His, not ours, and just as long as we abide we may trust Him fully to continue to undertake for us."

In spite of the intensity of the battle during the first six months in Carnot, the most significant struggles still lay ahead. First came the sad news that Myrtle Mae Snyder had died. Although she had left them in Brazzaville to assist another mission, they always assumed one day she would rejoin them in Oubangui-Chari. For two years she labored faithfully as a nurse and evangelist in a local mission hospital. But after a brief struggle with malaria, Myrtle Mae died on August 28, 1920. She was the second casualty of the pioneer team.

And more trials were just over the horizon. Some months earlier, James had written, "Resolute and zealous young men, as you only too well know, are at a premium and should be prayed to the field as soon as possible. Yet they should bear in mind that they will have experiences awaiting them which will try their souls as they have never been tried before. And it is only those who are absolutely determined to go through with God who will actually succeed. Nothing is more pitiful than a defeated missionary. . . . Alas, there are not a few." Little could James have anticipated that Antoine would become one of the "defeated missionaries." Not long after Myrtle Mae died, he announced plans to return to America.

October 11, 1920 was a bittersweet day for the pioneer team. Early that morning boats arrived with long-awaited supplies, some of which had been delayed almost three years in transit. But every box was broken, and many items lost or stolen. About 80 percent of the powdered milk and 90 percent of the flour was spoiled. Yet at least some supplies had arrived, bringing a degree of relief to the team.

Later that day, on the same converted whaleboats, Antoine, Marie, and Julia began the long journey back to America. Settling into life at Long Beach, California, Antoine would soon remarry. In 1924 he died from pneumonia, undoubtedly weakened by his trials in Africa.

Years later, reflecting on the departure of Antoine, Florence offered this gracious perspective: "Let no one judge the one who thus sadly returned to the homeland in discouragement and defeat because he had lost all hope that permission to evangelize Oubangui-Chari would ever be granted to the party. Let those who have followed a loved companion to the grave and have known the loneliness of a severed life, the anguish of a broken heart, and that upon the mission field, where even families often suffer from isolation, and where the solitary, especially the bereaved, enter into depths of suffering insupportable except through super-abundant grace—let those, and those only, judge him."

The next blow would strike even closer to home. Within months, Florence fell ill and once again seemed on the brink of death. While she would recover, the lengthy physical, mental, and spiritual strain was taking its toll on James. He confessed, "I am breaking. First my body weakens, then my nerves. . . . I ask for an increased amount of prayer." Yet with characteristic faith, he continued, "But I believe that we are just on the eve of victory, and the impulse of permission may be so great as to make a new man of me. . . . How great is man's work in this wild country where all is wilderness . . . especially if that man be alone."

Within two months, God finally answered those prayers.

Respond
For those who go:

1. With what you've learned about the circumstances surrounding his departure, would you have supported Antoine Rollier's decision to return to America? Why or why not?

2. Concerning Antoine, James later reflected: "Whatever has been the outcome of his coming to the field with his family, I do not believe that it was a mistake or in vain. For a very little while

and in a very unique way God greatly used him in Brazzaville. The fact that French was his mother tongue was certainly a great help." As you consider missionaries who have cut short their deployments and returned home, is your heart filled with compassion or judgment? Why?

3. Is it possible you're harboring resentment toward someone you view as a "defeated missionary," having "put his hand to the plow and turned back?" In light of today's reading, is God calling you to think and act differently toward them? Is there an action step toward reconciliation you should take today?

For those who send:

1. What do you consider to be legitimate reasons why a missionary would leave their field of ministry? On what do you base those reasons? How might the case of Antoine Rollier and the response of the Gribbles help you develop a more Christ-informed response?

2. Recognizing that you may never fully understand their reasons for leaving the field, take time to pray for ex-missionaries in your sphere of influence. Ask God to complete the work He desires to accomplish in their lives, bringing healing where needed, restoration of relationships (if needed), and guiding them into fruitful ministries in their home countries.

CELEBRATING ANSWERS TO PERSEVERING PRAYER

PERMISSION GRANTED TO EXPLORE OUBANGUI-CHARI,
BEGINNING FEBRUARY 2, 1921

Come and see what God has done:
he is awesome in his deeds toward the children of man.

PSALM 66:5

Left: James prepares to depart Carnot and scout out a suitable location for the new mission station. He traveled over one thousand miles on bicycle and by foot during his fourteen-week tour. *Right:* Porters assist James by carrying his supplies.

Read: Psalm 66

Reflect

As February 2, 1921 dawned over Carnot, Florence was suffering from yet another fever, one that would last unabated for seventy days. Food was still scarce. An active five-year-old, Marguerite required education, constant care, and creative activities to keep her occupied. Once again, promised reinforcements were delayed and one hundred miles still stretched between the pioneer team and Oubangui-Chari.

But this day would be different. The Governor-General was in town and wished to speak with James. As the conversation wandered from one topic to another, James worked up the courage to ask if permission had finally arrived from Paris. But before he could speak, he heard words he would never forget. "Where will you go, Monsieur Gribble, *now that you have permission?*"

Barely able to restrain himself, James wisely replied, "Where would the Governor like me to go?" After a long pause, the Governor replied, "How would you like to locate near Bozoum?" Again, James could hardly contain his excitement. Years before, as he daily poured out his heart over a map of Oubangui-Chari, his eyes inevitably rested on one place: Bozoum! Soon a telegram was speeding its way to America: "BRETHREN, ASHLAND, OHIO, ETATS UNIS. PERMISSION GRANTED. HALLELUJAH. LOCATING FURTHER INLAND. PSALMS 66 AND 126. GRIBBLE."

While another attack of fever would delay his departure for three weeks, James soon pushed forward with preparations to scout out a favorable location for the first mission station. With a horse, his bicycle, and thirteen porters, he said goodbye to Florence, Estella, and Marguerite. On February 26, 1921, he finally entered Oubangui-Chari!

Writing Florence regularly, James was careful to provide detailed records of his travels, including descriptions of the topography and population, records of his interactions with government and tribal officials, and even helpful information about customs, available food, and more. Everywhere that he traveled, he encountered open doors to share the gospel. And on many occasions, he employed his limited knowledge of medicine to bring relief to the local population.

"If you were to see the need of the Gospel in this country as I do," he wrote Florence, "the greatness of the country, and the absolute density of the spiritual night, you would not wonder at the opposition of the adversary. But we believe and trust God that by His grace

He will give us the very desire of our hearts, that of seeing the Gospel go forth in this land in great power. This field is so great that it is like a small world by itself. We will have no neighbors, as far as missionaries are concerned. . . . Keep looking up and trusting Him. The fight is hard but we have a God who holds us in His hands. It is His battle, not our own. We have nothing to fear."

Having suffered much in Africa from poor living conditions, James was committed to finding the ideal place for the new station. Good elevation would place them above the mosquito line. A healthy water supply would help prevent many waterborne diseases. There should be enough space to allow ventilation between buildings. And soil must be adequate for growing vegetables and fruit.

But health wasn't his only concern. "On my trip I had passed over much beautiful and well-watered country on the other side of Bozoum, but where were the people? It was for the people that we had come to Africa. So once more I earnestly cried to the Lord to show me His place for the mission station, telling Him it was His work, not mine. Then He led me to consider again the many things in favor of Bassai. . . . More and more He enabled me to believe that it was the very place where He would have us open a mission station."

He continued, "The Karre people are absolutely virgin soil. Islam has found no foothold there. . . . I certainly believe that Bassai is the very place to which God would have us go now. There are so many people within access even now. They will be within very easy access when the roads are once built."

Respond

For those who go:

1. Note how James wrestled with finding a suitable place for the mission station, even passing over some desirable locations because they were not close enough to his target group.

Assuming you had a say in your choice of housing, what criteria did you employ? Are you pleased with your choice? Is it time to make a strategic change?

2. What practical advice would you give a new missionary seeking housing? Do you feel your advice would make sense to James Gribble? Why or why not?

3. "Answered prayer seems most sweet when long-delayed." Has this been your experience? Why not take a moment to bask in those "big prayers" God has answered in your life?

For those who send:

1. One of the most meaningful ministries in which you can engage and one of the most helpful for the missionaries in your sphere of influence is *persevering prayer*. Do you have a list of the truly big items for which missionaries are praying? If so, how often do you pray through that list?

2. Why not reach out today and ask a missionary to share their biggest possible prayer needs? Then place those needs where you can remember to pray for them on a regular basis!

STICKING TO THE BASICS OF THE CHRISTIAN LIFE

EXPLORING OUBANGUI-CHARI, APRIL AND MAY 1921

Therefore, brothers, be all the more diligent to confirm your calling and election, for if you practice these qualities you will never fall.

2 PETER 1:10

Left: In this early photo of Bassai Hill, the "x" marks where James wished to establish the mission station. He hoped the higher altitude would place the missionaries above the mosquito line. *Right:* The village located at the base of Bassai Hill. James looked for a healthy location close to the local population.

Read: 2 Peter 1:3-11

Reflect

James had been gone about two months when Florence came face-to-face with what she considered her greatest trial yet. She had been struggling unsuccessfully to overcome another bout of malaria. By early April, it deteriorated into blackwater fever, a rare and often fatal complication where red blood cells burst, contaminating the blood and urine streams. Florence needed to return to America for appropriate treatment and rest. What's more, she was convinced she must place little Marguerite in an American school.

In her own words, it seemed God was marking out "a path so difficult that she herself never could have chosen it; one in which to walk necessitated a deepening of faith and a doubling of consecration. For it requires a greater courage and a deeper faith to humbly say, 'Thy will be done,' to realize the necessity of going aside for a time from the path of ardent service, than it requires to actively and earnestly *do* the Master's will." For a season, she reasoned, God was calling her "to be a passive rather than an active instrument in Oubangui-Chari's evangelization."

James and Florence had been faithful in exchanging letters, so he had kept abreast of the ups and downs of life at Carnot, including her many health challenges. But nothing could have prepared him for this news. Even so, we see a growing maturity in his reply. "The Holy Spirit has been saying many things to me since I left Carnot. Yes, it is even more important to say, 'Thy will be done,' than to be at the forefront doing His will. Yet those who must resignedly say, 'Thy will be done,' are the most obedient also. I have great peace . . . as the Lord whispers it is His work, not mine."

Back at Carnot, Florence was slowing recuperating and once again could assist Estella with the ministry. In a letter to James, she described a typical day: "We are continuing our study of Karre. Already we have a vocabulary of 600 words and have made a number of translations of Scripture portions, as well as a consecutive Gospel Story." She continued, "The days seem full. We have medical work, school with little Marguerite, Baya translation, and a Karre Class, all in succession following our morning devotions, breakfast, and prayer. . . . We preach a great deal in Baya. . . . As we long for you we would do nothing to hurry you to us. I have had no fever to speak of for nearly six weeks."

In a letter sent to a spiritual mentor in America, dated May 14, 1921, James provides a glimpse into his soul. "I have just had a most blessed season of prayer and am so thankful for the promises of the

Lord," he wrote. "This morning His message to me is, 'The eyes of the LORD are toward the righteous and his ears toward their cry' (Psalm 34:15). Yea, unto the righteous, but who am I that I should claim the promise? Like David, my sin is continually before me. Could I claim that promise?

"Yes," he continued, "I always claim it, do claim it, and have made my requests accordingly. I HAVE A RIGHTEOUSNESS that will stand before the bar of God; not my own, but imputed to me, and making me heir of His promises. How glad I am for Jesus and His finished work on Calvary's cross! I have laid my hands on the sacrifice and have acknowledged that He died for me, for my sins, past, present, and future. . . . May I more and more be given faith and grace to lay hold on the precious promises."

Respond

For those who go:

1. If not careful, we might fall into the trap of thinking that James and his teammates constantly faced dramatic events and heroic choices. Today's reading reminds us how much of missionary life is a daily struggle of obedience in mundane matters: preparing meals, caring for children, prayer, study, and meeting the spiritual, emotional, and physical needs of those around us. What's been your attitude recently toward the daily, mundane tasks God places before you?

2. James wrote, "The Holy Spirit has been saying many things to me since I left Carnot. Yes, it is even more important to say, 'Thy will be done,' than to be at the forefront doing His will. Yet those who must resignedly say, 'Thy will be done,' are the most obedient also." How might you express these thoughts in your own words? And can you illustrate them from your own experience?

3. Whether making heroic choices, being faithful with the "mundane" or learning to say, "Your will be done," James reminds us, "The Lord whispers it is His work, not mine." How might you apply his words to strengthen your resolve to be faithful in the tasks you face today?

For those who send:

1. Many of the hours in a missionary's schedule are filled with the tasks that never appear in a prayer letter or video to partners back home. They include maintaining a home, preparing meals, caring for children, prayer, study, exercise, and more. Take time to pray that God would grant energy and discipline for the missionaries to neither neglect nor overemphasize these important matters.

2. What do you think James wished to communicate to us when he observed, "It is even more important to say, 'Thy will be done,' than to be at the forefront doing His will"? How might his words help you maintain a healthy balance between prayer and action?

REGAINING A SENSE OF URGENCY

SAYING GOODBYE TO FLORENCE, MARGUERITE, AND ESTELLA,
MAY 31 TO JUNE 25, 1921

How are they to believe in him of whom they have never heard?
And how are they to hear without someone preaching?

ROMANS 10:14

Left: One of the final photos James would take of little Marguerite before she returned to the USA for her schooling. *Right:* James sharing the gospel with a village leader, believed to be Chief Sanga.

Read: Romans 10:5-15

Reflect

James estimated that the unevangelized region of Oubangui-Chari covered 225,000 square miles, approximately the landmass of the present-day state of New Mexico. He was convinced the task of evangelizing such a vast area could occur only as native workers were mobilized from local tribes and supported by local funds. Earlier he had written, "As soon as we organize our churches in Oubangui-Chari, we trust that they will be self-supporting. We expect to work for self-support for the native evangelists from the time that we have our very first churches. But the missionaries in Africa will always have to be supported from the home base."

Now he wrote, "The success of a missionary today in Africa is not to be determined by the number of years of service which he has had, nor the hardships he has endured, nor the number whom he has added to the church roll, nor by his popularity as a speaker or writer, but by the number of competent native LEADERS whom he has discovered and trained and put to work for the Master."

But with news of Florence's impending return to America, James knew it was time to draw his investigative trip to a close. During their fourteen-week separation, he had traversed over one thousand miles on bicycle and by foot. With much knowledge gained and many relationships forged, James felt ready to begin the evangelization of unreached tribes.

"However trying separations may be to the flesh," he observed, "there are times when they must be made, and under the most difficult circumstances, but when we place our loved ones in His hands He is faithful and just and will do that which He could not and would not have done had we refused to obey Him."

James arrived back in Carnot on May 31, 1921. Within hours, Florence once again fell ill and suffered greatly for five days. But by June 13 she was strong enough to travel and it was time to say goodbye to the city they had called home for eighteen long months. They would avoid the sweltering heat by using converted whaleboats to travel by night. To circumvent the rapids, local porters carried Florence in a special chair, Estella rode horseback, Marguerite on "native-back," and James on bicycle.

Soon, James was holding his five-year-old daughter tightly, not knowing it was the final time he would see her. It was June 20, and the two ladies and child were preparing to board a small steamer headed to the coast.

As they disappeared downstream, James slowly turned to begin the lonely journey northward to Bozoum. Stopping at each village to share the Good News, he later recorded this encounter with one of the native chiefs: "After telling to Chief Sanga the story of Jesus and how He died for our sins, I paused. He said, 'Tell me the story again.' I did so. When ready to leave, the chief asked to know more of the Gospel. . . . I asked what he particularly desired to know. He said to me, 'You tell me about being saved by Jesus, that He died for our sins, and that by believing on Him we can be saved and go to the place that He has prepared for us in heaven. *What about the Baya who have died without ever having heard the Gospel Story?'*

"Never was a question put more pointed or more forcefully. You know the force of such a question. Because of it, may there be an exodus of missionaries from America to Africa. . . . What was I to say? There he sat, staring me in the face and commanding an answer. Whom was I to indict? Surely not God, for He gave His Son that the Baya might be saved. Of course, I could not say that his ancestors would be excused because of ignorance. . . .

"I told him that God is a God of love and is faithful. I very force-fully told him that now after once hearing we will certainly be punished if we reject Jesus. . . . As I bade him farewell, Chief Sanga's eyes were filled with tears and he could not speak for emotion."

Respond

For those who go:

1. St. Francis of Assisi is often quoted to remind us of the need for good works to accompany the Good News: "Preach the Gospel every day. And if necessary, use words." Yet in today's passage, Paul states, "How are they to hear without someone preaching?" How do you define preaching in your context? Are you pleased with the way you are currently balancing "good deeds" and "preaching the gospel?"

2. Paul continues, "And how are they to preach unless they are sent?" (Romans 10:15). Let's pause for a moment to thank God for "senders." Are we doing enough to remind them of the critically important role they fulfill not only in our lives but also in the overall plan of God for the salvation of His world?

3. And finally, Paul reminds us, "How beautiful are the feet of those who preach the good news!" (Romans 10:15). Have you paused recently to honestly and sincerely and humbly thank God for granting *you* the immense honor of going? Why not do so now?

For those who send:

1. How did you feel when reading the question asked by Chief Sanga: "What about the Baya who have died without ever having heard the Gospel Story?" How would you have answered him?

2. And how did you feel when reading the words James sent to his partners in the homeland: "Never was a question put more pointed or more forcefully. You know the force of such a question. Because of it, may there be an exodus of missionaries from America to Africa!" Might God be calling *you* to form part of the next wave of missionaries? Why or why not? Are you willing to openly discuss your answer with a trusted spiritual advisor today?

REVIEW

The hut in this photo, believed to be that of a village witch doctor, serves as a solemn reminder that "we do not wrestle against flesh and blood" (Ephesians 6:12).

Today is your opportunity to review the Bible passages, reflections, and applications from the past week.

For those who go:

1. What is the primary spiritual lesson you feel God wants you to apply in order to reshape the way you think and serve as a missionary?

2. Is there a specific action step from your reading and reflection that you've postponed? Will you take it today?

For those who send:

1. What is the primary spiritual lesson you feel God wants you to apply in order to reshape the way you think and serve as a person who partners with missionaries?

2. Is there a specific action step from your reading and reflection that you've postponed? Will you take it today?

BEING CONTENT WITH THE ROLE GOD ASSIGNS

SEEKING PERMISSION TO BUILD WHILE WAITING FOR RECRUITS,
JUNE 25 TO SEPTEMBER 29, 1921

*What then is Apollos? What is Paul? Servants through whom
you believed, as the Lord assigned to each.*

I CORINTHIANS 3:5

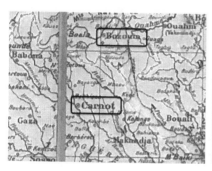 

Left: The approximately one-hundred-mile journey between Carnot and Bozoum took
about three weeks. Bassai Hill is not far away. Reinforcements would take the easier
route via Bangui, located at the extreme right about a fifth of the way up the map.
Right: Camping during the long journey back to Bassai.

Read: 1 Corinthians 3:5-15

Reflect

"Never fret about your lot," James wrote from Carnot, "for it may
be a precious jewel wrapped up in a gunny-sack, 'glory in disguise.'
God is faithful and has called us to a wonderful work. My share may
be the building of houses while others reap the rich harvests. God
will lead. If only this country is speedily and effectually evangelized
for Him, I will be content."

It was June 25, 1921, just five days after saying goodbye to Florence, Estella, and little Marguerite. Arriving back at Carnot, James was genuinely surprised at the warm welcome he received. Upon his departure two weeks earlier, most of the population had disappeared into the bush. James was relieved to discover they were merely following a tribal custom. It was considered inappropriate to mourn in public. But he had returned, and they were anxious to make clear how much they valued the presence of the missionary team, once again urging him to establish a permanent presence in Carnot.

But his sights were fixed northward on other unreached tribes. "The salvation of these thousands upon thousands of people is weighing more heavily upon me," he wrote, "and I believe that God is revealing a part of His plan to me. True, we may not be able to follow up those who are converted and baptized, but we know One who can. It is simply to obey the orders of that One that we are here."

On July 20, along with twenty-seven porters and a wagon, James once again left Carnot and began the arduous journey to Bozoum. Leaving fifty-seven additional loads at the government Poste, he gave instructions to forward them as soon as practical. Progress would be painfully slow. Frequently they were forced to use machetes, picks, and shovels to carve a road through the dense underbrush. Finally arriving on August 1, James was pleased to find two small houses built according to his instructions, providing a welcome change after so many nights of camping. On his first trip he'd commissioned these simple structures with the hope they would one day house the recruits he believed would soon arrive. But by August 15, he was pressing onward to Bangui in hopes of obtaining final government permission to establish a mission station at Bassai.

"We fully realize that all cannot go," he wrote from Bangui to William Gearhart at the home office, "and we are exceedingly thankful for those who, like yourself, carry such heavy burdens for the work at the home end of the line. God certainly will reward you and you will have a share in the glory when we, seated with the King, see the redeemed from dark Africa come marching in. Doubtless the burden will seem heavy at times, but push on with that renewed courage which the Lord shall give you."

To a candidate for the work, James wrote, "Do not be afraid of burying your talents. . . . Thanks be to God that through Him there is a resurrection of one's talents. We seemingly bury them in our love for God. He always resurrects them and they blossom out far more gloriously than if they had not passed through a death and a resurrection. Therefore, fear not, but rather rejoice over the privilege of making a complete and entire surrender to God. Remember, 'He is faithful.' Had I all the talents that God can bestow upon a human being, I would lay them all at the feet of Jesus. Nothing was too great for *Him* to leave for me."

James would delay his departure from Bangui for three weeks in hopes that promised recruits would soon arrive. We can imagine his disappointment upon learning they would be delayed yet another four months. Facing the prospect of carving out a mission station without the help of teammates, he penned one of his most revealing insights. "I am convinced of this," he wrote, "God is not going to look us over for medals, degrees, or diplomas, but for scars."

Respond

For those who go:

1. James recognized how God in His wisdom assigns different tasks to different workers. Take a moment to reflect upon the men and women upon whom your ministry depends. Who are they and how do their assignments differ from yours?

2. In today's Scripture reading, Paul not only teaches that God assigns us different roles, he also declares that it is "God

who gives the growth" (1 Corinthians 3:7). How should this truth impact the way you view your current assignment? The assignments of others?

3. Paul also explains how "each will receive his wages according to his labor," not according to his fruit (1 Corinthians 3:8). After all, it is God Himself who assigns some to plant, some to cultivate, and some to reap the harvest. Why not take a moment to thank Him for being such a fair and benevolent Lord of the harvest?

For those who send:

1. The letter James sent to Mr. Gearhart at the home office serves to remind us that missionaries on the front lines depend upon others who serve in support ministries. He wrote, "we are exceedingly thankful for those who, like yourself, carry such heavy burdens." Can you imagine what those "burdens" might be? How are they similar to or different from those of missionaries deployed on the front lines?

2. Do you know the names or functions of the men and women who serve the work of missionaries in your sphere of influence by serving at the home office? Why not send them a note of encouragement and thanks today? And be sure to pray that God would grant them the same power and perseverance as those serving on the mission field.

NAVIGATING THE TENSIONS BETWEEN FAITH AND WORKS

INITIAL WORK ON THE NEW STATION AT BASSAI HILL,
SEPTEMBER AND NOVEMBER 1921

So also faith by itself, if it does not have works, is dead.

JAMES 2:17

Left: Having obtained official permission to establish a station at Bassai, James pitches his tent onsite for the first time. *Right:* The initial group of workmen hired to clear land and construct roads and buildings. Several were later baptized.

Read: James 2:14-26

Reflect

"If we are to win in this field," James mused in a letter written while still in Bangui, "it must be through faith and the working of the Holy Spirit. We are going to the very forefront of the battle line. The crisis will never be over until the coming of our blessed Lord. We will always have to advance on our knees against what might be termed 'insurmountable difficulties,' with an implicit faith and trust in God and His Holy Word."

"How good it is to know," he continued, "that we have a God who is absolutely faithful and who never gives a call or a command without

the enabling. Therefore, when he said, 'Go therefore and make disciples of all nations,' He also said, 'And behold, I am with you always,
to the end of the age.' Over and over again God has made it clear and
plain that this is His work, and that He is directing it. There is a part
for us to play in it, to permit ourselves to be used as instruments in
His hands. Yesterday I did nothing but pray. I literally spent the day
in prayer, as I felt that we are facing a crisis in the work."

On September 23, James finally received the long-awaited verbal
permission to establish the first mission station. He departed Bangui
on September 29, stopping for a short visit at Bozoum, then arriving
at Bassai Hill in early November. By November 7, James deployed
the first native workmen to begin clearing brush and leveling the
ground. On November 9, he pitched his tent. For the first time,
James could call Bassai his home.

Today, it's nearly impossible for us to imagine the ingenuity and
pure grit required of pioneer missionaries called upon to carve out
viable living spaces where everything must be shipped from far away
or made from the materials at hand. We vividly see this challenge
as James tackled the task of surveying the site for the new station.
Unwilling to use meager ministry funds to purchase surveying equipment, he pressed forward with materials on hand. "I used a pocket
compass, an inverted aluminum cup, an empty oatmeal tin, a table,
a pair of opera glasses, and native assistants who had not the slightest
idea of what I was trying to do! . . . My measuring line was a rope."

Although French government officials were only permitted to
live two years in the region, missionaries expected to stay as long as
health allowed. With a realistic understanding of what was required
for Westerners to survive in the heart of Africa, James knew that the
location of the mission station was among the most important decisions he would make.

"When we trust God in a matter," he observed, "things always
turn out better than we think. When searching a site for a mission

station last March, it seems God spoke to me, and told me this was the place. So I trust Him concerning it. It is His station. I am grateful for good water, good clay, good timber, and that we are able to burn some of the rocks."

Days were filled with essential yet mundane tasks like measuring and laying foundations, burning bricks, cutting timber into usable boards, and more. "I am writing you while overseeing men, working at four jobs, and while buying grass, poles, and bark for tying purposes. I now make several hundred purchases a day in addition to my other work."

One of the primary challenges of effective cross-cultural ministry is learning to balance faith and works. James pursued that balance, as illustrated in this comment: "I find that in order to get the work done satisfactorily, I must spend much time in prayer and be very strict with the men. The road must be built, a workshop must be erected, a sawing shed also; the chickens must be cared for and housed."

Respond

For those who go:

1. One of the greatest challenges of the Christian life is to find and maintain a healthy balance between faith and works, prayer and action. Are you satisfied with that balance in your life? Why or why not? In what ways might the example of James help you maintain a better balance?

2. What lessons from your personal journey might you use to help a younger, less experienced missionary maintain a healthy equilibrium between prayer and action?

3. Take a moment to review your schedule for the past two weeks. Does it reflect the balance you described above? Now turn your thoughts to next week. What adjustments might you make to better reflect that balance?

For those who send:

1. In the opening paragraph to today's reading, James describes the need to "advance on our knees against what might be termed 'insurmountable difficulties.'" Select one or more missionaries from your sphere of influence and attempt to list their insurmountable difficulties. If you can't identify them, why not ask?

2. What would it be like to "advance on our knees" with them? Why not spend time literally on your knees interceding for these men and women today? How did this experience help you identify more closely with the challenges they are facing?

SURVIVING LONELINESS

LABORING WITHOUT TEAMMATES AT BASSAI,
SEPTEMBER THROUGH DECEMBER 1921

*He gives power to the faint,
and to him who has no might he increases strength.*

ISAIAH 40:29

Left: Boulders presented the first big challenge. The smaller ones were buried and the larger heated until they cracked. *Right:* Lumber had to be cut onsite. Soaking it in a stream for 30 days helped prevent destruction by insects.

Read: Isaiah 40:25-31

Reflect

"The Lord is with us even though the devil is against us," James wrote shortly after saying goodbye to Florence and Marguerite. "The fighting is fierce, and as I am the only missionary in these parts, I can expect the brunt of the battle. But the presence of the Lord is very sweet and precious. In that Name, the Name above every name, we will triumph." It was July and he was still at Carnot, making preparations to relocate to Bassai and confident that reinforcements would soon arrive. Little did James know those reinforcements would be delayed until late December. He would spend the next six months alone.

Long delays in sending and receiving mail added to his sense of loneliness. "I was sorry to receive word in this mail that my mother is far from well," he wrote from Bassai on November 15. "I may never see her again in the flesh. But because of the matchless grace and sure salvation of the Lord I shall see her, for she is one of His own looking for His coming. . . . How I do thank our dear Lord for His finished work and for the Blessed Hope." Yet his mother had already passed away on August 25, almost three months before news of her illness reached him.

As Christmas approached, James was feeling an acute need for contact with the outside world. "I will soon begin to wonder if I am on the earth or on Mars, or if the Lord has come and taken . . . His own . . . and has left me with the Karre and the Baya." Even letters written from nearby Bangui could be delayed two months in reaching Bassai.

"Well," he continued, "if I hear nothing from the outside world, and if missionaries are delayed, or if this party, like the others, fails to arrive, I will by the grace of God continue to open up this station, and get it in shape to accommodate missionaries. I know God answers prayer. It is His will that the land be evangelized and the church called out from these tribes. . . . He will not leave me alone."

And in a moment of deep transparency, James reflected, "The life of a missionary is a great life if you don't weaken. Not many of us can truthfully say we never weaken. But, thanks to God, there is One to whom we can always flee; a rock of strength and blessing in whom we can always hide. For my part, I confess that many, many times in my missionary life I have weakened and do weaken. . . . Oh, how thankful we are for a strong One upon whom we can lean. I certainly do sympathize with the new recruits who come to the field without having learned how to lean upon that One during stress and strain."

On December 23, James finally received the long-awaited news. Recruits would soon arrive in Bangui! In the meantime, however, and similar to his experience in Nera eleven years before, he faced the prospect of spending another Christmas alone, far from family and friends.

Several years passed before Florence took pen in hand to reflect upon the trials of separation and loneliness. Looking back upon 1921, she wrote, "None is more blessed than the missionary; none more happy than they who, obeying the Great Commission, find themselves in some lonely outpost, preaching the Gospel in the 'regions beyond.' On that last frontier, they hear the Master saying, 'And behold, I am with you always, to the end of the age'; and they become fully persuaded of the immutability of this and all His promises."

Respond

For those who go:

1. In today's Scripture reading, Isaiah addresses those who may feel abandoned by God—"my way is hidden from the LORD" (Isaiah 40:27). What truths about the nature and character of God does Isaiah reflect upon to answer this accusation?

2. When you feel most alone, what strategies do you employ to help you cope with loneliness? Are they effective? Are there insights from the lives of these pioneer missionaries that might help you cope better in the future? What are they?

3. In light of today's readings, what is God saying to you?

For those who send:

1. It's likely that every missionary experiences intense moments of loneliness, compounded by the distance that separates them from family and the support network of their home church.

Using the words of Isaiah 40:25-31 as your guide, pray that the missionaries in your sphere of influence would experience the realities of these promises today.

2. While the greatest need of a missionary is to find his or her encouragement in the promise that Jesus will be "with you always, to the end of the age," they also need encouragement from you. Why not take a moment right now to send a word of encouragement to a missionary in your sphere of influence?

MAKING CHOICES THAT IMPACT THE FAMILY

FLORENCE FINDS A HOME FOR MARGUERITE,
JUNE 1921 THROUGH FEBRUARY 1922

I will pour my Spirit upon your offspring
and my blessing on your descendants.

ISAIAH 44:3

The last known photo with the three Gribbles
plus Estella Myers.

Read: Isaiah 44:1-8

Reflect

Florence and Marguerite left Carnot on June 13, 1921, assuming they would quickly find passage on a ship bound for America. But they were delayed in Matadi for three months, finally setting sail on September 14. Arriving in New York in late October, Florence discovered her father had passed away twenty-five days earlier. Within less than a year, she had suffered the loss of both parents and her mother-in-law. "Seldom does the missionary return to find home circles unbroken," she later wrote, "although few enter so deeply into the fellowship of His sufferings as to sustain a triple bereavement on the very eve of arrival."

Florence and Marguerite soon boarded a train for Philadelphia, where the members of the First Brethren Church warmly received them. It was the very church where years earlier James had been baptized and trained for ministry. The congregation listened eagerly to reports and joyfully helped outfit Florence and little Marguerite with adequate clothing for the impending winter. Within days they were boarding another train for Long Beach, California, where Florence planned to meet with leaders of their mission agency, the Foreign Missionary Society of the Brethren Church.

With her health on the mend, Florence was now free to focus attention on her greatest challenge—how to provide for her daughter's future? The two months in Long Beach gave Marguerite her first opportunity to attend school, but this was only a temporary arrangement. What of a permanent home? Through a mutual friend, a childless couple in Sunnyside, Washington, learned of Marguerite and wrote with an invitation to consider them as foster parents.

Due to long delays in communication with James, Florence realized this was a weighty decision she must make on her own. After many inquiries, lengthy personal interviews, and creating space for Marguerite to bond with her potential "adopted parents," Florence reached her decision. She would leave Marguerite with the Weed family and continue her ministry on the East Coast. It was Valentine's Day, February 14, 1922. At the station, little Marguerite pressed a handmade card into her mother's hand. As the train pulled away, held high in the arms of her adopted mother, she cried out, "Look at me, mother, *just as long as you can*. . . . Just look at me the *last one!*"

"Must it ever be thus, this separation of missionaries from their children?" Florence reflected. "No, not always. There is only one *must* for the servant of God, 'This Gospel *must* be preached.' By the wooing and the winning of His own precious Spirit, by that tender witnessing within, which we know as spiritual guidance, God speaks to the parents when it is His will that a child should be surrendered. And not only that, but He provides a home for the child, and the grace for the surrender to His will."

It may be tempting to pass judgment on the decisions previous generations of missionaries made about their children. Florence warns us to avoid this mistake. "Let no one think that he or she can tread this holy pathway in any human strength. Let no one follow another in surrendering a child. Let no parent submit the decision to another. Not within one's self, nor in any other human source can grace be found for this greatest of human abnegations, the surrender of a child."

And Florence dreamed of a day when parents and children would not be forced to live on opposite sides of the world. "May the time soon come when in Oubangui-Chari, as in many other fields, schools can be established for missionaries' children, so that children's lives and parents' example may unite as an object lesson to native child-training. *Then* fathers and mothers need no longer suffer that most subtle of pains, the sight of their children's anguish. *Then* the tremendous risk of children being weaned away from that missionary career, which when educated upon the field they naturally and freely follow, need no longer be taken."

Respond

For those who go:

1. Today, missionaries have access to many options for their children's schooling. Yet sooner or later, separations must come. How might the truth of today's Scripture passage and the Gribbles' example help a missionary cope with these inevitable separations?

2. Florence warns us about passing judgment on decisions others make with respect to the schooling of their children. Have you fallen into this trap? How might you respond more appropriately in the future?

3. Why not take time right now to pray specifically for those facing family separations? Would you be willing to write them a note of encouragement?

For those who send:

1. Let's imagine Florence had the opportunity to speak into your relationships with parents or children. What do you think she would say? While you may not face the same big decisions as she faced, how does her example help you think more biblically about your most intimate family relationships?

2. Take a moment to pray specifically for those missionary families in your sphere of influence who are separated from parents or children. It's likely your list includes *all* the missionaries you know! Pray specifically that God would grant grace to not only endure periods of separation, but also to embrace those periods with the confidence that they are fulfilling God's good and acceptable and perfect will (see Romans 12:2).

REJOICING IN FIRSTFRUITS!

REINFORCEMENTS ARRIVE AND NEW CONVERTS ARE BAPTIZED,
DECEMBER 1921 THROUGH JUNE 1922

For I am not ashamed of the gospel,
for it is the power of God for salvation to everyone who believes,
to the Jew first and also to the Greek.

ROMANS 1:16

Left: Orville Jobson performs the first baptisms of converts at Bassai. *Right:* Estella Myers tends to the sick.

Read: Romans 1:7-17

Reflect

It was a hot, sultry evening during the summer of 1921, and the leader of a small prayer meeting in Philadelphia was deeply burdened for James Gribble. Knowing James was alone, often ill, and facing tremendous obstacles, he earnestly urged those present to pray for God to raise up two men to join James as soon as possible. The meeting had scarcely concluded when young Orville Jobson spoke up: "I want to be one of those men!" By September 14, Orville was setting sail from New York to Africa.

Almost three years earlier, a young woman named Charlotte Hillegas also responded to the plea for more workers. Having arrived in France in May 1921, she was already heavily engaged in language study when Orville arrived.

By October, Orville and Charlotte were setting sail from France for Africa, taking full advantage of the more accessible and reliable route up the Oubangui-Chari River to Bangui. Arriving on December 12, they were warmly welcomed by Estella Myers. After departing Carnot in June and helping Florence and Marguerite set sail for America in September, Estella had attended a conference of Africa missionaries, then settled at Bangui to wait for the arrival of reinforcements. The three single missionaries arrived at Bassai on December 31, just in time to join James to "pray in" the New Year.

With companions now on site to work alongside veteran missionaries James and Estella, the new team soon completed three houses and several outbuildings. Yet much work remained. They needed to clear more land, extend roads, shape and bake bricks, cut and cure timber (they discovered that soaking lumber in a stream for a month would slow the destructive work of boring insects), and plant a vegetable garden and fruit trees.

As a nurse, Estella faced a constant stream of those urgently needing her assistance. Fellow medical missionary Florence understood the strategic role of medical work in pioneer missions. "Miss Myers was now busily occupied with medical work," she wrote, "especially caring for lepers and others greatly afflicted. Many were carried daily to the station for treatment. The medical work in a heathen tribe is one of the factors greatly used by the Lord Jesus in taking 'captivity captive' and revealing Himself in loving kindness to the heathen."

Although construction projects and medical ministries occupied much time and energy, the pioneer team was committed to pursuing their primary mandate: the evangelization of least-reached tribes.

On May 28, 1922, they celebrated the firstfruits of their labors as nine men and two women from the Baya, Karre, and Boufi tribes were baptized. Two more Baya and another Karre were baptized the following Sunday.

"The native Christians," James had written two years earlier, "those who have been born again, are the joy of the missionary and his crown. But the winning of souls is no easier here than at home. When converts are made in a land like this, one experiences a surprising joy. No living being upon earth can have greater joy than to be used in leading souls to the Lord Jesus from among a people who have never previously known of Him."

The missionaries were eager to organize a Communion service with the twelve new converts. "Last night," James wrote a day later, "we could hear, far into the night, the natives singing Gospel hymns in the valley below; which is quite a contrast to the dance song which we usually hear on moonlight nights."

"Concerning evangelism, more and more the blessed life-giving Gospel is being faithfully preached in these mountains. Today Mr. Jobson and the native Christians are out on a definite campaign to every village within miles of here. Miss Myers and Miss Hillegas preach the Gospel faithfully in the nearer villages. So far we have no vehicle suitable for their reaching the more distant ones."

Following the example of James, who years earlier found his bride on the mission field, Orville soon proposed marriage to Charlotte. They married on November 19, 1922 and served together more than four decades in central Africa.

Respond

For those who go:

1. Most missionaries would agree with the statement "God cares about the entire person, body and soul." The challenge, however, is to hold these two priorities in creative tension,

resisting the temptation to overemphasize either present or eternal needs. Do you feel you and your teammates are succeeding in managing this tension? Why or why not?

2. Take a moment to reflect on the words of John Piper, which he shared at the Lausanne Conference in Cape Town, South Africa (2010). Does his perspective help you better manage this tension?

> Could Lausanne say—could the evangelical church say—we Christians care about all suffering, especially eternal suffering? I hope we can say that. But if we feel resistant to saying "especially eternal suffering," or if we feel resistant to saying "we care about all suffering in this age," then either we have a defective view of hell or a defective heart.

3. As James observed, "those who have been born again . . . are the joy of the missionary and his crown." Has God granted you that joy? Whether you're engaging directly or indirectly in harvesting spiritual fruit, take a few moments to bask in the joy of conversions to Christ.

For those who send:

1. Throughout the modern era of missions, medical workers have built significant bridges into least-reached people groups by caring for the entire person—body and soul. Today, we often refer to this as "holistic ministry." But this isn't limited to the field of medicine. Take a moment to consider the missionaries in your sphere of influence. Can you affirm and celebrate additional ways they are seeking to minister to the entire person?

2. Four years and four months passed between the moment the pioneer team set sail (January 1918) and the moment they celebrated their first baptisms (May 1922). In a world that often expects or demands quick results, how does this sobering reality help modify the expectations we place upon our missionaries? How might the example of these pioneer missionaries help you rethink your expectations?

SUBMITTING TO HUMAN GOVERNMENT

JAMES REFLECTS ON CIVIL RESPONSIBILITIES,
FROM 1915 THROUGH 1922

Let every person be subject to the governing authorities.
For there is no authority except from God, and those that exist
have been instituted by God.

ROMANS 13:1

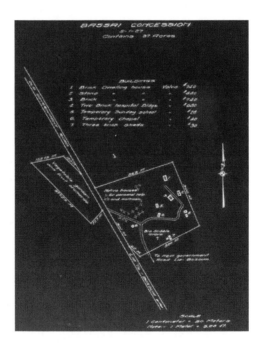

Every aspect of land development and construction
required additional permission from French officials.

Read: Romans 13:1-7 and Titus 3:1-2

Reflect

The lengthy and convoluted road to obtain permission to enter the heart of Africa began during the three long years James and Florence spent in America. Countless letters were carefully composed, translated, and sent to the colonial governments who controlled each of the territories they would traverse. "We are finding it hard," James wrote, "to meet all the requirements of all the various governments whose shores we must touch, British, Belgian, and French. But praise the Lord, the God in whom we trust can roll back all opposition."

Yet in spite of their best efforts, upon arriving in Africa the pioneer missionaries still lacked final permission to enter the Oubangui-Chari region, which they learned had to come from Paris. Control of the region had only recently passed from the Germans to the French as part of the peace treaty that brought an end to World War I. Much infrastructure had been destroyed, lines of communication were painfully slow, and many government departments were still rebuilding. And although relations between France and the USA were friendly, the French struggled to understand and accept that American missionaries were not official agents of the state church and government.

Even with permission papers in hand, the pioneer team continued to face many cultural misunderstandings and government red tape. "I was surprised to find that the Administrator had a question to raise about the concession request," James wrote, "saying that there was a flaw in it. Of course, in all deliberations I try to be very humble and submissive, for this is God's work and not mine, and all undertakings must be by Him and not by me." And we sense Gribble's frustration as he continued, "I find that separate requests must be submitted for each form of missionary enterprise. Having obtained the concession, we must now go through the prescribed formula for the obtaining of church, school, dispensary, etc."

These experiences help remind us that mission work doesn't take place in a vacuum. Ever since Jesus first gave us the Great Commission, cross-cultural workers have faced the reality that human governments hold the power to either facilitate or impede our ministries. Navigating the requirements for obtaining visas, permissions to rent or purchase properties, and authorizations to hold religious meetings can tax the patience of even the most committed missionaries. And this assumes we are welcome where we minister, which frequently isn't the case when serving among the world's least-reached people groups.

Working with government officials can create high degrees of anxiety and stress. The unfamiliar regulations and sometimes capricious expectations placed upon missionaries can be fertile ground for criticism, frustration, and even efforts to circumvent the law. In most cases the question isn't *whether* we will face these challenges, but rather, *how we will respond to them.*

Let's allow James to speak into this matter. "Nothing must deter us from obeying the Great Commission of the Risen Lord who is with us to see the campaign through. However we must also, as we are taught by the same Lord, walk carefully and obediently before Him as far as the Governments of this world are concerned, and expect Him, as we wait upon Him and trust in Him, to cause these very powers that be to do His will."

During the thirty-six months from his first meeting with the Governor-General in Brazzaville until he was finally authorized to enter Oubangui-Chari, James had relentlessly prayed for God to move the hearts of French government officials. Even with permission in hand, another seven months would pass until he received authorization to begin construction on the mission station. And with construction underway, James continued his efforts to foster the goodwill of the French and gain the favor of local African leaders.

Then came very exciting news. Florence was returning!

Respond

For those who go:

1. We recognize the Enemy opposes our work and can channel that opposition through the corruption and injustices we experience at the hands of government officials. Yet we must avoid the temptation "to see a demon in every delay, denial, or dismissal" as we learn to navigate government regulations in contexts where we lack a complete understanding of the culture. What advice would you give to a new missionary who is growing frustrated with what he or she sees as government red tape?

2. What are practical ways you have learned to show "respect to whom respect is owed, honor to whom honor is owed" (Romans 13:7), even when their actions frustrate your plans?

3. Paul instructed Timothy to pray faithfully for those in government so "that we might lead a peaceful and quiet life, godly and dignified in every way" (1 Timothy 2:2). Is this a part of your regular prayer routine? How might you pray for those in authority over you today?

For those who send:

1. Before you take time to intercede for missionaries who face the challenge of respecting and honoring the governments where they live and serve, take a moment to reflect upon your own attitudes in light of today's Scripture passages. Is the Holy Spirit convicting you of areas in which you fall short of

God's will for you? If so, take time to confess this as sin and to commit to demonstrating a truly biblical attitude toward those God has placed in authority over you.

2. Now you are in a great place to intercede for the missionaries in your sphere of influence. Taking into account that most of them are working in countries where government regulations do not favor church activities or mission work, ask God (a) to move in the hearts of government officials to facilitate and not impede the work of the Great Commission, and (b) to grant patience and perseverance as missionaries attempt to navigate a myriad of new cultural expectations and complex legal requirements.

REVIEW

Young men and women enjoying a local dance.

Today is your opportunity to review the Bible passages, reflections, and applications from the past week.

For those who go:

1. What is the primary spiritual lesson you feel God wants you to apply in order to reshape the way you think and serve as a missionary?

2. Is there a specific action step from your reading and reflection that you've postponed? Will you take it today?

For those who send:

1. What is the primary spiritual lesson you feel God wants you to apply in order to reshape the way you think and serve as a person who partners with missionaries?

2. Is there a specific action step from your reading and reflection that you've postponed? Will you take it today?

RESPONDING TO LOSS

FLORENCE RETURNS WITH A PROMISING NEW RECRUIT,
NOVEMBER 3, 1922, THROUGH JANUARY 17, 1923

*For I know that my Redeemer lives, and at the last he will stand
upon the earth. And after my skin has been thus destroyed,
yet in my flesh I shall see God.*

JOB 19:25-26

Above: Allen Bennett enjoys an opportunity to
spend time with African children and young people.
Right: James erected a temporary grave marker until
something more permanent could be ordered.

Read: Job 6:1-10 and Job 19:23-27

Reflect

From almost any angle, Allen Bennett seemed an unlikely candidate
for missionary service in Africa. With a somewhat underdeveloped
physique and frequent illnesses, his parents often wondered if their
son would survive until adulthood. What's more, his family relocated
several times, creating havoc with his education and delaying his
completion of grade school until age fifteen.

But the most significant setback came a year later while traveling to a family funeral with his grandfather, aunt, and mother. A speeding train struck their car at "Death's Crossing," killing the others and carrying Allen more than six hundred feet before the locomotive could stop. Allen would spend the next twelve months recuperating in the hospital. Bones were set, broken, and reset, and a steel plate inserted to stabilize his leg.

Two years later, he was back in the hospital for more surgery. Taking a particular interest in him, a young nurse challenged Allen to think beyond his limitations and consider how God might use him as a foreign missionary. Yet it was the death of another nurse, pioneer missionary Myrtle Mae Snyder, that moved Allen to consider joining the missionary team in Oubangui-Chari. After graduation from high school at age twenty and a short stint in the workforce, Allen was ready to take concrete steps to turn his convictions into reality, enrolling for classes at the Bible Institute of Los Angeles (BIOLA).

It didn't take long for Florence to come to admire the young man. "Allen Bennett is a young Hudson Taylor," she wrote James. "He travels third class because there is no fourth; dines on next to nothing, or forgets to dine at all; yet has wonderful provision from the Heavenly Father for every actual necessity." After studying French in Europe for six months, Allen was ready to join Florence as she set sail for Africa.

While the journey from Europe to Bangui took only three weeks, compared to more than three years for the original missionaries, it had its share of significant challenges. The ship from Europe to Matadi was broadsided in the fog and nearly capsized. The smaller steamboat in which they sailed up the Congo River caught fire, which was providentially doused by a heavy rainfall that sprang up within the hour. But an even bigger challenge was Allen's health. He was frequently ill. At one point, Florence decided she must move him ashore to recuperate, not knowing how they would later proceed to

Bangui. Imagine their grateful surprise at the unexpected appearance of another boat that was willing to take them aboard.

James was waiting for their arrival in Bangui and quickly developed a deep bond with Allen. Perhaps, he wondered, this was the son for whom he had always longed? But as they set out for Bassai on December 18, 1922, Allen's frequent fevers and weaknesses continued. By January 8 his fever spiked to 106 degrees, forcing them to take refuge at the tiny village of Gazeli.

Suspecting he had contracted Spanish influenza, they quarantined Allen in a little hut to protect the local population. For ten long days Allen hovered between life and death. His final intelligible word was "better," and on January 17, 1923, he passed into God's presence. Due to fear his illness might spread, they buried him within hours and burned his hut to the ground.

Of all the significant trials they faced over the years, the loss of Allen seemed to impact the Gribbles most deeply. "Dr. Gribble and I both feel that we have never before been so deeply bereaved as when Mr. Bennett went from us," James mused. Yet, "we bow our knee to His sovereign will which is as high above ours as the heaven is high above the earth. Allen Bennett knew depths of suffering such as few of us have ever fathomed."

Among the many letters of consolation that poured in over the following weeks was this note from a fellow missionary: "We shall never know why his life was taken when there is such a need of workers. But we all came to the mission field asking that whether in life or in death we might glorify the Master."

Respond

For those who go:

1. Allen Bennett "seemed an unlikely candidate for missionary service in Africa." Yet the annals of mission history are full of such candidates, while perhaps many considered "more

suitable" were unwilling to go. In which category might others place you? Can you describe how the obedience of the "less suitable" might bring greater glory to God?

2. Today's Scripture reading runs counter to the increasingly common belief that God intends to grant his children a meaningful, relatively pain-free life. How might Job's experiences help us counter that storyline in our lives and ministries?

3. What is God saying to you today about the important roles that pain, death, and separation play in our pursuit of the Great Commission?

For those who send:

1. Let's reflect upon the important role of the nurse assigned to care for Allen Bennett. While meeting physical needs is a noble and necessary ministry, she also cared about his spiritual needs and even challenged him to pursue missions. Is God calling you to fill a similar role in the life of another "Allen?" What concrete step could you take today to help a young person consider becoming a missionary?

2. Go back and read again the final paragraph of today's story. From a human perspective, the death of Allen Bennett would be labeled "untimely." Using what you know about the Old Testament character Job, what words of encouragement would you have written to James and Florence in their moment of grief?

OVERCOMING BETRAYAL

THE TEAM FACES MAJOR TRIALS AT BASSAI,
FEBRUARY TO MARCH 1923

*You keep him in perfect peace whose mind is stayed on you,
because he trusts in you.*

ISAIAH 26:3

Yama and his wife were young workers
and converts from the Boufi tribe.

Read: Isaiah 26:1-9

Reflect

James and Florence arrived at Bassai on February 6, 1923, grieving
the loss of Allen Bennett yet grateful they were finally together again.

Both had suffered illnesses during the trip, with James wondering at one point whether Florence would be the fourth pioneer missionary to be buried in African soil. But her strength was slowly returning, and they were eager to join Estella Myers and the newly married Jobsons in the many tasks that lay ahead.

But only two weeks passed until they were severely tested again. The roots of this story stretch back to late 1920 or early 1921, when a young man from the Boufi tribe named Yama first offered to help the missionaries. He proved to be a capable worker, and the missionaries soon invited Yama and his wife to live among them. James grew to trust him deeply and even left him in charge of the station during his fourteen-week scouting expedition into the Bozoum region. Later Yama accompanied James to Bassai and often encouraged him during the long months he was separated from all contact with Westerners. So no one was surprised when Yama and his wife were among the first to be baptized and to join the infant church at Bassai.

But a personal tragedy precipitated his tragic downfall. During October 1922, Yama and his wife celebrated the birth of a son, only to mourn his death a few days later. In typical tribal fashion, they assumed a person caused his death and soon fixed the blame on Bengai, another worker whose wife had also given birth to a baby boy. So intense was the hatred and so real the threats that the young mother and son were forced to flee the station.

All seemed to return to normal for a time. But one night the mission storehouse was robbed, and Yama was quick to single out Bengai as the guilty party. As Bengai was led off in chains, the soldiers also forced Yama to come along as a witness. Details are sketchy, but by morning the soldiers returned, convinced instead that Yama was the real culprit. Escaping into an inner room where Florence was once again in bed with a fever, Yama armed himself with a knife and threatened to kill anyone who approached. This standoff lasted forty-eight hours until the soldiers finally stormed his stronghold. Armed with a spear and knife, Yama fought viciously until a chance opening permitted him to escape through a window into the nearby bush.

Within the hour, the storeroom was ablaze, and the missionaries suffered significant losses. Fearful Yama would attack again and conscious that other buildings might burn, they huddled together for protection in the Jobson home. Native believers quickly volunteered to protect them, although James insisted that they lay down their spears and stand guard only with their shields. Days passed with no resolution. All work was temporarily suspended. Unable to bear the tension and heat any longer, the missionaries finally abandoned the sweltering house and made feeble attempts to resume their normal activities.

This sense of being "under siege" stretched over several weeks until one day they were awakened by a cry from high on an overlooking rock. "I want to see Bembo," Yama shouted, using James' local name. Ignoring the pleas of his teammates, James determined to face the armed and starving Yama without protection. But God had already done His work and the young man was waiting to surrender. He had come to plead with James to provide him safe passage to the regional official, without which he faced almost certain death at the hands of the frustrated soldiers. Yama was later tried, found guilty, and sentenced to twenty years in prison.

But the story has an amazing and unexpected ending. Long before Yama completed his sentence, he was released from prison. As a symbol of his personal transformation, he took the new name "Paul" and went on to become a faithful deacon in the newly established church in nearby Yaloke.

Respond

For those who go:

1. Let's take a moment to empathize with the pioneer missionary team on at least two levels:

    a. First, attempt to feel the high drama and uncertainty they experienced for several weeks as Yama was loose in the nearby bush. While circumstances are certainly different, have you experienced similar moments in your life and ministry? How did you cope? What might you do differently when called upon to face such moments in the future?

    b. Next, attempt to identify with their sense of disappointment as a promising young convert fell into sin and took steps to harm his missionary mentors and friends. Have you experienced something similar with young converts or trusted national partners? How did you cope? Where did you find consolation? What did you learn about God, yourself, and your ministry values that might help you successfully navigate such a challenge in the future?

2. What are practical ways you might combine your personal life experiences with the promise of Isaiah 26:3 to help others navigate moments of high drama, uncertainty, and disappointment?

For those who send:

1. Few are the pioneer missionaries who escape the disappointment of seeing early converts abandon their new faith and fall back into old habits and lifestyles. While such circumstances are always difficult to understand, they are especially hard

to accept when one has labored long and hard, and when spiritual fruit seems so scarce. Today, we invite you to pray that God would protect from discouragement the missionaries in your sphere of influence, even when their "firstfruits" prove unfaithful. Feel free to adapt these powerful words as part of your prayer: "You keep him in perfect peace whose mind is stayed on you, because he trusts in you" (Isaiah 26:3).

2. Now we invite you to turn your attention to those converts who may have fallen away. While it's unlikely you know their names, this doesn't prevent you from praying for them. Taking encouragement from the fact that Yama was ultimately restored to Christ, the church, and the missionaries, pray for God to do a similar work in the lives of others who have fallen away.

DAY 38

ACCEPTING THE ULTIMATE SACRIFICE

JAMES AND HIS FINAL ILLNESS, FROM MARCH TO JUNE 4, 1923

For to me to live is Christ, and to die is gain.

PHILIPPIANS 1:21

Only five years after his arrival in central Africa, and a little over two years after permission was granted to occupy Bassai Hill, James Gribble passed to his eternal reward, the fourth pioneer missionary of his team to die.

Read: Philippians 1:18-30

Reflect

With Yama safely in custody, James was free to rejoin his teammates. Soon they were making good progress on all fronts, as witnessed by the Kardaals, a couple from America who visited Bassai: "Building a new station among a primitive people like the Karre is no easy task. It takes strength and patience. But the work is in fine progress, and the missionaries have found willing hands for work. At that time buildings, large and small, were under roof, and several others were under

146

construction. The Gospel was preached, the sick were cared for, the language was studied. A place of rocks, thornbushes, and trees was under conversion into gardens, roads, and building lots. The natives were all impressed by the material aspect of the work, and some were spiritually influenced. Prayer and praise were the keynote sounded by the missionaries. . . . We congratulate you indeed for the splendid opening your work has made in the Karre mountains."

In his annual report James rejoiced in spiritual fruit. Writing on April 30, 1923, he described six major evangelistic campaigns into neighboring districts, resulting in thirty-seven converts baptized during the previous twelve months. And although still lacking a permanent dispensary, a steady stream of patients received medical treatment six days a week.

Lasting fruit usually comes at a high cost, however, and intense spiritual conflicts were always boiling just beneath the surface. In a rare moment of transparency, James wrote, "I did wrong to permit myself in any wise to be moved by any of these things. I should have gone on trusting the Lord just as if nothing had taken place. I have great peace constantly in knowing that both the work and the policy adopted for it are of God. . . . May I continually appropriate more grace. . . . We look for the Lord Jesus to see the travail of His soul and be satisfied. That is to be our reward. Otherwise I do not see how we could stand here for a moment!"

As the day dawned on May 31, 1923, the mission station was a beehive of activity, with construction projects underway, patients to attend, an evangelistic service to conduct, a multitude of smaller chores to complete, and, as always, letters to write. James was feeling a particular sense of urgency to complete more buildings as they expected five recruits to arrive soon. Although weakened by months of labor mixed with illness, he was determined to press on.

But by that evening, he felt the familiar chill and his temperature soon climbed to 102 degrees. It was the painful start to yet another bout with blackwater fever, that extreme malarial condition that often claims the lives of its victims. As his health steadily deteriorated over several days, James seemed to accept that his end was near. At one point he sang out in a clear, sweet voice:

My Jesus, I love Thee, I know Thou art mine—
For Thee all the follies of sin I resign;
And say when the death-dew lies cold on my brow;
"If ever I loved Thee, My Jesus, 'tis now."

These words had never held such meaning before. Calling Florence to his bedside, he whispered, "I am ashamed to be so happy when I am leaving you in this world of suffering. But I commit you unto God."

James would linger for another two days, slowly slipping into unconsciousness as his body struggled to cling to life while his spirit was yearning to be free. That moment of freedom finally arrived at 10:55 p.m., June 4, 1923. With the final words, "Come, Lord Jesus," he became the fourth of the pioneer missionary team to be buried in African soil.

Sometime later, Florence drew a connection between this experience and the words of the great missionary François Coillard: "Pray for me that I may be faithful to my Master, and faithful unto death," he wrote. "Pray, oh, pray, all and earnestly, that He may grant me the joy of seeing my ministry close only with my death. My great, great desire is not to live a day longer than I can work."

Respond

For those who go:

1. Take a moment to read again the words of Coillard. Do you agree with his perspective on life and ministry? Why or why not? How might you rephrase his thoughts in your own words?

2. One of the many spiritual descendants of James Gribble was the Chadian evangelist and church planter, Dadje Samuel (1962–2010). Used of God to help launch a church planting movement in eastern Chad and beyond, he penned these words a few months before his untimely death: "Each missionary being sent out is signing his death sentence. He must have a very close relationship with God because his days are numbered. Those with a half-hearted commitment cannot do the work." In practical terms, what does it mean for a missionary to "sign his death sentence?" Have you signed that "death sentence?" Why or why not?

For those who send:

1. In today's Scripture reading, Paul expresses optimism that God will deliver him from his current trials "through your prayers and the help of the Spirit of Jesus Christ" (Philippians 1:19). Take a moment to reflect upon the dual roles of the faithful prayers of Paul's ministry partners and the intervention of the Holy Spirit. How do these words encourage you to continue your ministry of intercessory prayer for missionaries?

2. After James' death, Florence found much consolation in the words of another pioneer missionary who wrote: "My great, great desire is not to live a day longer than I can work." These words would seem quite strange to those whose primary goal is to only work long enough to retire, then live for pleasure the rest of their days. How might God desire to use the examples of Gribble, Coillard, and Samuel to inspire you to "let your manner of life be worthy of the gospel of Christ" (Philippians 1:27)?

DAY 39

REFLECTING ON COSTS AND REWARDS

FROM PIONEER FIELD TO WORLD'S
MOST EVANGELIZED REGION

*You have been grieved by various trials, so that the tested genuineness
of your faith—more precious than gold that perishes though it is tested
by fire—may be found to result in praise and glory and honor
at the revelation of Jesus Christ.*

I PETER 1:6-7

Left: Lester Kennedy was the fifth pioneer missionary buried in African soil in November
1931. *Middle:* Florence Newberry Gribble continued to serve faithfully as a missionary
doctor and evangelist until her death in Africa in March 1942. *Right:* Three tribal chiefs
burn their amulets in a public demonstration of faith in the God preached by pioneer
missionaries.

Read: 1 Peter 1:3-13

Reflect

By 8:00 the following morning, James Gribble was carefully laid
to rest in a makeshift cemetery on Bassai Hill. His grave lay within
the borders of the mission station he had so carefully surveyed less
than two years earlier. Estella was already on her way to America and
would not receive news of his death for several weeks. Also ignorant

of the news were the five new recruits just setting out from Bangui to Bassai: John and Carrie Hathaway, Chauncey Sheldon, Florence Bickel, and Minnie Deeter.

For her part, Florence Gribble was determined to press on. Remarkably, within seven months she would join the Hathaways in establishing a second mission station in the strategic center of Yaloke, about 120 miles away. As replacements poured in over the next few decades, more stations were established, untouched regions evangelized, believers discipled, leaders trained, and churches planted, until one day this region would be declared among the most evangelized on the globe!

It is good to pause to ask the question, "At what cost?" By 1931, Lester Kennedy had died, becoming the fifth casualty of the work and giving the mission the rather unenviable honor of losing one of every five recruits.

Still, they came. All suffered, most adapted, and some stayed long enough to see the fruit of their labors. Many returned to America after long years of service with their health broken beyond repair. And only God knows the exact number of those who died due to the diseases and infections they carried home.

Of those buried on African soil, we honor two precious missionary children, Philip Beaver (1953) and Serge Aellig (1966), along with the following adults:

Mary Ganshorn Rollier, of malaria, September 16, 1919
Myrtle Mae Snyder, of malaria, August 28, 1920
Allen Lee Bennett, of Spanish influenza, January 17, 1921
James Steinhaur Gribble, of malaria, June 4, 1923
Lester W. Kennedy, of cancer, November 5, 1931
Florence Newberry Gribble, of fever, March 3, 1942
Joseph H. Foster, of causes unknown, March 2, 1951
Estella Myers, worn out from years of ministry, November 1, 1956
Janet Varner, of causes unknown, November 6, 2015

Seldom remembered, however, are the less tangible costs. How many families in America celebrated births, baptisms, weddings, and funerals *with an empty chair*, placed in honor of loved ones serving in Africa? How many aging parents longed to see their children *one more time* before leaving this world? How many children *wished they could consult Mom and Dad* about big life decisions, knowing that distance and slow communications made such discussions impractical? And how many grandchildren only knew Grandma and Grandpa *through pictures, stories, and very occasional visits?*

Turning now to more concrete statistics, during the first one hundred years of missionary activity in central Africa, Encompass World Partners deployed more than two hundred workers who served at least two years or longer. Their combined service adds up to more than 3,450 years of intensive labors (and only God knows the number who served on strategic short-term assignments!). While it's nearly impossible to calculate the financial contribution of the small denomination that sponsored the work, in today's money we estimate they sacrificially gave more than $250 million.

But ultimately, does "cost" really matter? Charles Yoder, pioneer missionary to Argentina, had sent these words of encouragement as the team still waited for permission to enter Bozoum: "Livingstone was buried in Africa but his life stirs all Christendom. And you, dear comrades, are few . . . but your light shines on and is helping to transform not only Africa but the church at home. What a joy to be thus doubly useful! In our field there is no sacrifice to be compared with the joy of shining like a little candle in the great dark night, but far more useful thus than an electric light shining amid a thousand others."

Respond

For those who go:

1. In "man's economy," ROI (return on investment) serves as a major benchmark to determine how, when, and why we invest. Reflecting upon what you've discovered or rediscovered about missions through the life of James Gribble, what would you describe as the principal benchmarks in "God's economy?"

2. Today, we have the privilege of looking back over one hundred years of ministry in the central region of Africa, and few would question whether the sacrifices of our missionary team were "worth it." If you are serving in a "historic field," take a moment to thank God for the sacrifices of those who came before you. And if you are among the first to arrive among a least-reached people group, take courage! While it may be years before an abundant harvest, know that you are investing your life into something truly meaningful, truly eternal!

3. Charles Yoder wrote about the unique joy of missionary work as "shining like a little candle in the great dark night . . . far more useful thus than an electric light shining amid a thousand others." Rejoice in the honor of being a light in a dark place! And know that we deeply appreciate you!

For those who send:

1. It shouldn't come as a surprise that there is some question about whether sending missionaries to foreign lands is "a good investment." Reflecting upon what you've discovered or rediscovered through the life of James Gribble and his team, how might you help someone understand that missions is more than ROI (return on investment)?

2. Some of the "unsung heroes" of missions are the parents, grandparents, and children who willingly release their loved ones to the mission field. Who does this include in your sphere of influence? In addition to praying for them today, is there a concrete way you can reach out and thank them for their sacrifice?

Special Note: As Florence features so heavily in our story, it's appropriate to add this interesting epitaph, written upon her death in 1942 by missionary doctor Floyd Taber. "She was one whose whole life had been a giving of herself over unto death; who had always sought the hard places; who for years had remained in this earthly tabernacle only by virtue of the resurrection life. She had so many mortal ailments, and still lived on, that people sometimes wondered if the ills were not partly imaginary. But, after repeated medical examinations, I *know* they were very real. When dealing with a miraculous life, you can't follow the same rules as in ordinary cases."

HONORING THE INDISPENSABLE ROLE OF WOMEN

A TRIBUTE TO ESTELLA MYERS AND THE WOMEN WHO FOLLOWED HER

I have fought the good fight, I have finished the race,
I have kept the faith.

2 TIMOTHY 4:7

Left: Estella Myers, one of the original four pioneers, served thirty-eight years in central Africa until her death in November 1956. *Middle:* "We spent Sunday at Chief Iremo's and listened to his pleading for his people, the Banou, until I was ashamed to say I was on the way home," Estella wrote in her diary as she prepared for her first furlough in 1923. *Right:* Estella is buried in the small cemetery on Bassai Hill.

Read: 2 Timothy 4:1-8

Reflect

Women are often the unsung heroes of the Great Commission. Yet without their sacrifice, perseverance, talents, and grit, how much could men like James Gribble accomplish what they did? During the first one hundred years of ministry in central Africa, 60 percent of the staff deployed by Encompass World Partners were women. In most cases, these hardy souls shouldered the same burdens as their male counterparts and frequently were called upon to make even greater sacrifices. In their honor, we share the story of one of their best representatives.

Estella Myers was a member of the original pioneer party. Her thirty-eight years of service illustrate the best qualities of the women who followed the trails she blazed. James Gribble, knowing firsthand the value of his teammate, penned these words as Estella prepared for her first furlough: "She is beyond doubt one of the greatest and most self-sacrificing missionaries that we have ever had the privilege of laboring with. May God give us more of such."

As a young woman, Estella burned with ambition to make a name for herself. Happy to leave the family farm in a forgotten corner of Iowa, she set her sights on becoming a professor of mathematics. But within a year, the long hours and self-imposed stress combined to cause a nervous breakdown. Estella was forced to abandon her dream and once again take up residence on the farm.

As she slowly battled her way to better health, most friends believed Estella was home to stay. After all, they reasoned, her weak disposition and newly acquired speech impediment severely limited her options. Imagine their great surprise when she announced plans to study nursing and become a missionary, later joining the Gribbles on their pioneer expedition to central Africa.

During her almost-forty-year deployment, Estella learned to say "yes" to many assignments, whether or not she deemed herself qualified. She served as nurse, teacher, translator, construction supervisor and worker, children's worker, missionary stateswoman, speaker, and recruiter.

But above all, Estella was an evangelist, a fact amply confirmed by the extensive evangelistic tours she organized during the early years at Bassai. At first, her arrival at a new village was usually met by fear and opposition. Yet more often than not, Estella's tiny frame and nonthreatening manners opened doors, perhaps in a way a man could not. And, like the rest of us, she learned much through trial and error. Filled with prophetic condemnations of pagan practices, her first messages typically produced hostility and open resistance. But when she learned to focus on the love and compassion of God, barriers came tumbling down, hearts were moved, and repentance invariably followed.

It was shortly into her second term when Estella accepted another challenge. New believers required training, yet the Bible was not yet in their language. Who could address this pressing need? In typical fashion she threw herself wholeheartedly into the daunting task of translating the New Testament into the Karre language, even taking time to study Greek at Grace Theological Seminary and translation theory with Wycliffe Bible Translators. Upon completing the Karre New Testament, she turned her attention to a translation for the Pana tribe, a project Estella was still pursuing when she died.

Single missionaries, both men and women, tend to struggle with loneliness on the field, and Estella was no exception. She would struggle with these feelings during her entire career; a condition made more difficult when female companions would marry or leave the field. In her own words, "Being alone at times grips me, but after all it is not being as brave as I should that really pains my heart." Twice she was courted by eligible missionary men, and twice she said "no" to marriage proposals.

So perhaps it is fitting that Estella was alone when she passed peacefully into God's presence on November 1, 1956, seventy-two years old and still laboring. She was laid to rest on Bassai Hill, in the small cemetery shared with James and Florence Gribble. Undoubtedly Estella would have been quite pleased to hear the words of Jean Noatemo, an African colleague who tutored her in local dialects and later assisted her in translation work: "She had the body of a white man but the heart of a black man."

Special Note: When commenting above that 60 percent of our deployed staff to Africa were women, this statistic only includes those who served a minimum of two years. Of course, many stayed for decades. The exact statistics at time of publication were 118 women and 82 men.

Respond

For those who go:

1. As a single missionary, Estella provides a glimpse into the unique challenges faced by those missionaries, male and female, who choose to remain single for the sake of the gospel (see 1 Corinthians 7:7-8). If you are a single missionary reading this question, what do you wish your married colleagues better understood about the unique role of single missionaries in missions?

2. Estella also provides insight into the challenges faced by women on the mission field. While often called upon to sacrifice in ways similar to their male counterparts, many also fulfill unique roles as spouses and mothers. And many face cultural biases and prejudices that add significant weight to the other burdens they bear. If you are a woman reading this question, what do you wish your male counterparts better understood about the unique role of women in missions?

3. Do you agree or disagree with this statement: "Women are often the unsung heroes of the Great Commission?" What concrete steps might mission agencies and churches take to better affirm the sacrifice and commitment of women? Would you have the courage (and tact!) to share those insights with someone in leadership today?

For those who send:

1. Take a moment to identify the single missionaries in your sphere of influence, attempting to put yourself in their shoes. What might be some of the unique challenges they face? After thanking God for their ministries, consider whether there might be specific ways you could affirm and encourage them today.

2. Now consider missionary women who have invested their lifetime in missions, whether single or married. Take time to thank God for each of them. Then select one to be the object of your affirmation and encouragement. How might you reach out to thank her today?

DAY 41

GAINING AN ETERNAL PERSPECTIVE

CELEBRATING OVER ONE HUNDRED YEARS OF SPIRITUAL FRUIT!

They will bring into [heaven] the glory and the honor of the nations.

REVELATION 21:26

Left: Orville Jobson preaches at one of the early outdoor services on Bassai Hill, with Estella Myers looking on from the portable organ. *Right:* Florence Gribble seizes an opportunity to share the gospel during a roadside stop.

Read: Revelation 21:22–22:6

Reflect

It was 1909, and with less than a year of missionary experience in Africa, James was already pleading for God to release him to labor among the yet unevangelized tribes of the interior. Little did he know the years of sacrifice that lay ahead, and even less could he imagine the fruit that would come from his efforts. Instead, he chose to focus on the *privilege* of serving as a pioneer missionary. "As I push on from one pioneer field to another," he wrote while still in Kijabe, "I will not ask for a seat at the right hand or left hand of Jesus in Heaven—I will only ask to sit at the gate and see the redeemed of the Lord come

160

in from those parts of Central Africa where I have been privileged to be a pioneer missionary."

By 1932, Florence had successfully captured the story of James' life in a 400-page book entitled *Undaunted Hope: The Life of James Gribble.* As his journals and extensive correspondence are lost to us, we are deeply indebted to Florence for our primary source material for this book. Fewer than ten years had passed since his death, yet already Florence could document progress among the Basakuma and Akamba of Kijabe (Kenya), the Kikuyu and Agikuyo of Nera (Tanzania), and several tribes near Gacengu (Uganda), people groups among whom he labored while with the African Inland Mission.

Of course, James would be the first to insist the glory goes to Jesus Christ and the many missionaries who have built upon the foundations he helped lay. But let's imagine for a moment that God granted his request "to see the redeemed of the Lord come in from those parts of Central Africa" where he labored. What might he be celebrating at this moment?

In the central region of Africa where he served, conservative estimates place the current number of churches tracing their direct spiritual ancestry to James Gribble at 3,500. Assuming an average attendance of one hundred adults, membership must number at least 350,000. Yet average attendances of city churches are much higher, often numbering in the hundreds or thousands. And should we attempt to count non-baptized children . . . you get the idea!

Currently, the highest concentration of these churches is located in the western section of the Central African Republic (CAR), not far from the long-abandoned mission station at Bassai. The second highest concentration lies to the north in neighboring Chad. Both countries once formed part of French-controlled "Oubangui-Chari" and were granted independence shortly after World War II.

But the story of growth continues. By the 1980s, church members seeking to improve their economic prospects began migrating from the CAR and Chad to neighboring Cameroon, where they formed dozens of immigrant churches. Today, they are taking concrete steps toward assuming responsibility to make disciples among the Cameroonian population that surrounds them.

Meanwhile, African leaders in the CAR and Chad have seized the opportunity to deploy church planting teams southward into the two Congos, northwestward into Nigeria, and eastward into Sudan. And faithful to the convictions of their spiritual father, all churches and pastors are supported by local funds.

As the African church has evolved, so has the mission agency that gave it birth. Currently Encompass World Partners cooperates with national churches to support nine Bible schools, two graduate-level seminaries, and a host of decentralized leadership training initiatives. In the medical realm, the hospital founded by Florence Gribble still cares for patients at Yaloke (CAR) and a dental clinic provides relief to many in Bangui (CAR). A successful surgical center in Gadjibian (Chad) will soon be joined by another in Roro (Chad). Managed fully by Africans, these centers also provide a steady stream of income to help underwrite evangelistic outreach efforts. Dozens of dispensaries are staffed by trained nurses who also serve as evangelists, often providing the only medical care accessible to the local population. And in the educational realm, future leaders of government and business in the CAR receive training in our high school, while dozens of church-based grade schools provide primary education for thousands of orphans. To the north in Chad, new grade schools and health clinics are strategically placed to strengthen pioneer church planting efforts by creating "Christian infrastructure."

Should God grant James Gribble his desire to sit and see the redeemed enter heaven from the fields where he was a pioneer missionary, *he is a very busy man, indeed!*

Respond

For those who go:

1. For agencies like Encompass World Partners, the chapter of *Pioneer Missions* in regions like central Africa has come to a close. We've passed to the chapter of *Partnership Missions*. How might you describe the differences in missionary activity and attitudes between these two chapters?

2. How might national believers answer the same question? Are you on the same page? Why or why not? What steps might you take in the immediate future to open fresh paths of dialogue through which this question can be honestly considered and appropriately answered?

3. One of the greatest motivations for James Gribble was his deep conviction that he had "read the final chapter" and knew with certainty "how the story ended." In other words, he took great comfort in how the book of Revelation describes the eternal state as one in which representatives from all tribes, tongues, and nations will populate heaven. Take a moment to worship God in faith for this reality and reflect upon how it encourages you to remain faithful and focused on your tasks today.

For those who send:

1. Have you considered the final chapters of Revelation and the indispensable place of *the nations* (read: ethnic groups) in heaven? As the apostle John labored to describe our eternal state in words we might understand, he gave a prominent place to the multitude of ethnic groups that form part of the heavenly landscape. Considering how *ethnic differences* lie at the root of so many human conflicts today, how does this reality serve to make heaven an even more remarkable place?

2. The regional movement launched by James Gribble is impacting at least one hundred distinct ethnic groups today. Yet there are still hundreds more with little or no gospel witness. As a result of reading this book, will you commit to joining us in prayer daily that God will raise up more James Gribbles to share the Good News with them?

FINAL REVIEW

How then will they call on him in whom they have not believed?
And how are they to believe in him of whom they have never heard?
And how are they to hear without someone preaching? And how are
they to preach unless they are sent? As it is written, "How beautiful
are the feet of those who preach the good news!"

ROMANS 10:14-15

Today is your opportunity to review the Bible passages, reflections, and applications from the past week.

For those who go:

1. What is the primary spiritual lesson you feel God wants you to apply in order to reshape the way you think and serve as a missionary?

2. Is there a specific action step from your reading and reflection that you've postponed? Will you take it today?

For those who send:

1. What is the primary spiritual lesson you feel God wants you to apply in order to reshape the way you think and serve as a person who partners with missionaries?

2. Is there a specific action step from your reading and reflection that you've postponed? Will you take it today?

ACKNOWLEDGMENTS

I'd like to thank the Board of Directors of Encompass World Partners for insisting that I create space in my schedule to work on projects like this one, as well as the staff members who patiently carried on during those absences.

I'd also like to thank those who read early drafts and gave invaluable insights. These include but aren't limited to Sue Guiles (my wife and best friend!), Jesse Deloe (longtime friend and supporter of Encompass), and staff members Karen Foster and Louise Klawitter. In collaboration with the good folks at Tyndale House Publishers, who donated their services for text layout and cover design, Josh Feit helped shepherd the manuscript from Word Doc to its print ready format. And I must not forget Terri Carter, my assistant for many years, who covered for me during writing leaves and helped locate a number of photos that were 'lost' in our archives.

And I'm especially pleased to give a shout out to several passionate, younger leaders who graciously read and spoke into the final draft. They include Peter LeDuc, Sunni Gressock, Justin Mancari, Joy Martin, Chaim O'Deens, and Chad Painter. I love your passion for God and His mission!

TEXTUAL SOURCES

JAMES GRIBBLE kept diaries and took pictures, and we are grateful! Without those disciplines, I could never have written this book. While his original diaries are lost to us, we're really grateful to his wife, Florence, who painstakingly reviewed his journals and published his biography in 1932, less than ten years after his death. Most of the quotes in this book are taken directly from that biography and can be located by using the list on the next page. I also depended upon Florence to reconstruct important locations and dates, although this task presented more challenges than one might imagine. The few quotes from other sources are also credited below.

PRIMARY SOURCE

Gribble, Florence Newberry. 1931. *Undaunted Hope: The Life of James Gribble*. Ashland, OH: The Brethren Publishing Company (copyright by The Foreign Mission Society of the Brethren Church).

SECONDARY SOURCES

Gribble, Florence Newberry. 1950. *Stranger than Fiction: A Partial Record of Answered Prayer in the Life of Florence Gribble*. Winona Lake, IN: The Brethren Missionary Herald Company (copyright by The Foreign Mission Society of the Brethren Church).

Jobson, Orville D. 1957. *Conquering Oubangui-Chari for Christ*. Winona Lake, IN: The Brethren Missionary Herald Company.

Snyder, Ruth. 1984. *Estella Myers: Pioneer Missionary in Central Africa*. Winona Lake, IN: BMH Books.

Except where otherwise indicated, the quotes in this book are taken from Florence Gribble's book *Undaunted Hope*, on the pages listed below:

Day 1: 6, 161–162, 164, 276–777
Day 2: 9
Day 3: 16–17, 150
Day 4: 17, 26
Day 5: 29, 36
Day 6: 38–39
Day 8: 49–50, 63, 64–65
Day 9: 71, 75, 231–232
Day 10: 84, 83, 84, 84–85, 151
Day 11: 93, 109, 113
Day 12: 137, 114, 135, 136, 162, 139
Day 13: 165, 170, 138, 132, 145, 148
Day 15: 172, 175. For the Thomas à Kempis quote, see *On the Imitation of Christ*, book 1, chapter 19.
Day 16: 189, 191, 195–196, 196
Day 17: 204, 205, 110
Day 18: 214, 217, 221–222
Day 19: 223
Day 20: 222, 226
Day 22: 231, 223, 233–234, 240, 240–241
Day 23: 239, 242
Day 24: 244, 242, 249, 254, 277
Day 25: 268–269, 271, 272
Day 26: 279, 282, 282, 284
Day 27: 205, 278, 285, 290–291
Day 29: 294, 294, 299, 316, 298–299
Day 30: 300, 309–310, 310, 313, 312
Day 31: 294, 308, 312, 312, 313, 314
Day 32: 321, 325, 326, 326, 326
Day 33: 320, 210, 331, 335
Day 34: 163, 304–305, 330–331
Day 36: 341, 375–376, 378
Day 38: 394, 389, 398, 396
Day 39: 286–287
Day 40: For the quotes about Estella Myers, see Snyder, 132, 123, and Jobson, 147.
Day 41: 24

PHOTO CREDITS

Except where noted below, all photos are from original glass slides and belong to the archives of Encompass World Partners.

Day 1: Johnstown Trolley, circa 1905. Robert T. Rudge was the conductor, courtesy of P. Gary Burkett; early building of the First Brethren Church of Philadelphia, courtesy of Mike Taylor.

Day 2: Photo of the *St. Paul* under steam by John S. Johnston, photographer for the Detroit Publishing Company. Library of Congress, public domain.

Days 2, 11, and 15: 1909 Map of Africa by Sir Edward Hertslet (Map of Africa by Treaty, 3rd edition), public domain.

Day 3: Florence is pictured at her graduation from medical school in 1906; James is pictured upon arrival back in the USA in 1916, perhaps his earliest portrait on record; Mr. Hurlburt's photo cropped from a larger print that includes former president Theodore Roosevelt, public domain.

Day 4: The Kiambogo building at Rift Valley Academy, Kijabe, from approximately 1912, public domain.

ABOUT THE AUTHOR
AND HIS ORGANIZATION

DAVE GUILES grew up in the home of parents who "longed to go" on their own unique journey. Willing to quit stable jobs, sell their home, and say goodbye to a loving church family, his parents, Ron and Irene, became church planters in Pennsylvania and Texas, then concluded their ministry as a local church pastor and wife in Florida. This willingness to "go anywhere and do anything" for God deeply impacted their children and the legacy even extends to their grand-kids today.

Dave and Sue met at Grace College about the time God was reshaping Dave's career aspirations and calling him into full-time ministry. Once married, he enrolled in Grace Theological Seminary (Winona Lake, Indiana) with plans to become a pastor. But God had other plans, and soon Dave and Sue were sensing a call to make disciples outside of the relative safety and predictability of ministries in the USA.

During twelve years of cross-cultural labors in Buenos Aires (Argentina), Dave focused much of his energies on challenging traditional models of missionary work and church planting. In collaboration with local and international colleagues, he worked out the implications of doing cross-cultural ministry based upon New

Testament metaphors. Not only did this become the basis of his later doctoral studies, but more importantly, it empowered local believers to engage in frontline ministry without depending upon the special skills, training, and finances of Western missionaries. Contact Dave for more information about the Apostolic Church-planting Team Strategy (ACTS).

In 2000, Dave and Sue relocated to the headquarters of Encompass World Partners, where he became the youngest executive director in the agency's illustrious history, ushering in a period of significant changes designed to help a one-hundred-year-old mission adapt to the realities of a radically changing world. It also provided opportunities to collaborate closely with veteran workers while helping mentor a new generation of missionaries.

Dave and Sue currently reside near the Encompass World Partners headquarters in Atlanta, Georgia. They are parents to four children who are each working out the practical implications of God's call upon their own lives.

Encompass World Partners is the cross-cultural ministries arm of the Charis Fellowship of North America (charisfellowship.us) and partners closely with the global Charis Alliance (charisalliance.org). Currently, the agency deploys workers in eighteen countries and partners with the fruit of its labors in several more. Learn more at encompassworldpartners.org.